Decisive Battles
of the Civil War

Decisive Battles
of the Civil War

BY LT. COL. JOSEPH B. MITCHELL

With Thirty-Five Maps Designed by the Author

FAWCETT PREMIER • NEW YORK

DECISIVE BATTLES OF THE CIVIL WAR

Published by Fawcett Premier Books, a unit of CBS Publications,
the Consumer Publishing Division of CBS Inc.,
by arrangement with G. P. Putnam's Sons.

THIS BOOK CONTAINS THE COMPLETE TEXT
OF THE ORIGINAL HARDCOVER EDITION.

ISBN: 0-449-30836-7

PRINTED IN THE UNITED STATES OF AMERICA

21   20   19   18   17   16   15   14   13

To my wife, Vivienne
and to my children, Sherry and Brad

Contents

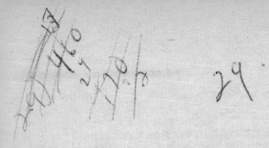

Foreword

THIS book has been written with two basic ideas in mind. The first was to present a short history of the Civil War with its events and leaders in their proper perspective. The second was to place its battles and campaigns in modern, up-to-date surroundings.

There have been hundreds of books written about the War Between the States. The student can find numerous thick volumes covering every phase of this great struggle. Many well-known authors have contributed excellent biographies of the important leaders on both sides. The battles and campaigns in both the East and the West have been studied separately and in great detail. Most of us, when confronted with such a vast wealth of material, find it difficult to keep the various events in their proper place in relation to the whole war effort. This book attempts to do so by subdividing the war into phases. The limiting points chosen were not calendar dates, but the decisive battles of the war. Nine progress maps, covering both East and West, were prepared to illustrate these chapters. To keep the scale of these progress maps within reasonable limits, events occurring too far to the west are not described nor are the naval battles that took place in waters too distant from our shores.

The second purpose of this book, to present the battles and campaigns in modern dress, is accomplished by using present-day road maps. At first, it was doubtful whether this could be accomplished with accuracy. The very latest maps obtainable from the government were carefully compared with those contained in the Official Records and other sources. Each of these in turn was studied on the ground, battlefield by battlefield. I soon found that actually the road system was the very best of guides. Of course, the curves had been straightened in many places, entirely new roads had been built, but time and again the old routes were still in existence either as paved roads or at least as trails.

My efforts to show always both old and new were, of course, impossible where cities had grown to engulf the battlefield area, or where the scale of the maps was such that differences could not be illustrated. The latter was true in the case of the campaign maps. Here I chose to continue to use modern maps, plotting the routes taken by the armies directly on the present-day road net where they coincided.

My hope is that with these maps the new developments, the new statues, roads, and buildings, will become aids to understanding what happened. I have used the present-day spelling of place names, noting in the text where the place names have changed so radically as to be unrecognizable. When a battle was fought on Southern soil, I have used the Confederate name; on Northern soil the name given to it by Union leaders has been adopted.

There have been two men who have guided me most in the preparation of this book. The first was my father, Brigadier General William A. Mitchell, who was Professor of Engineering and Military History at West Point. From him I acquired a liking for the study of military history, and I hope also some of his grasp of the subject and ability for portraying it in clear, understandable terms. I would like to think that this book carries on his work.

The second is Brigadier General Thomas North, now Secretary of the American Battle Monuments Commission. During World War II he was Chief of the Current Group, Operations Division, War Department General Staff. He was the officer primarily responsible for many of the great improvements made in the portrayal of combat action on maps. Having served with him on both the General Staff and the Commission, and having learned a great deal from him, I hope that the maps in this book will meet with his approval.

I am deeply indebted to Colonel Girard Lindsley McEntee who placed his entire unpublished manuscript, *Military History of the Civil War*, at my disposal.

Special thanks are also due to Mr. Erdmann Brandt, who showed a keen interest in this book even in its earliest days, and to Miss Lois Dwight Cole for her most helpful literary criticism, editorial advice, and encouragement.

I wish also to express my appreciation to Mrs. Edward V. Dunklee for lending me a complete set of the Official Records of the Union and Confederate Armies; to Mr. Edward Shenton, who contributed to the idea of writing this book; to Mrs. Ruth Talovich, who lent her artistic talent to the first of the maps; to Mr. Stuart Rose for criticizing parts of the manuscript; and to Miss Emily Johnson, who helped with some of the detailed research.

The employees of the National Park Service, particularly the cemetery superintendents and their assistants, were most helpful in my battlefield research.

Finally I wish to express to my wife, Vivienne Mitchell, my heartfelt appreciation and gratitude for her valuable criticism, suggestions, and co-operation in the preparation of this book.

J. B. M.

The Opposing Forces

AT 4:30 in the morning, Friday, April 12, 1861, a mortar shell burst squarely over Fort Sumter. The Confederate artilleryman who aimed this first shot of the Civil War must have been an expert gunner. It landed exactly on the center of the target, the Union fort in the harbor of Charleston, South Carolina. The results of the bombardment that followed can be compared only with "the shot heard 'round the world" at Lexington in 1775 and with Pearl Harbor in 1941. The people of the United States, both North and South, were instantly aroused to action. The long discussions, debates, and arguments of the preceding months and years were abruptly finished.

It is sometimes difficult for us today to understand why this war could not have been avoided. We now live in a united country. We have friends who come from all sections of our nation. We cannot conceive of any differences that might arise between two sections of our country that could be resolved only by war.

If, however, we try to imagine two distinctly separate nations constantly battling each other in the halls of Congress, we would come closer to understanding how divided the North and South actually were. When the thirteen original States joined together to form the Union, the North and the South were approximately equal in strength. Gradually, as the years passed, the States in the northern part received the bulk of the foreign immigrants. During this period most of the heavy industry became concentrated in the North, while the South remained largely agricultural with its economy based on the slave system.

As both North and South expanded westward, new States were admitted into the Union. Each of these allied itself with either the slave or the free States. It became a contest between the two economic systems. With its faster growing population, the North slowly and steadily grew stronger. The South soon realized that it could not hope to remain equal in the House of Representatives where representation depends on population; its only hope was to keep the number of slave and free States balanced so that it would remain on fairly equal terms in the Senate.

In the years preceding the Civil War many compromises were offered to try to maintain this equality. However, a strong feeling grew in the North among an increasing number of people that slavery was morally wrong and must be abolished. This feeling soon began to express itself in many ways, often violently. Naturally, the Southern people resented being told by the "abolitionists" how to run their own affairs. Many prominent Southerners realized that the slave system must come to an end, but they felt that they were better able to solve their own problems in their own way. A deep hostility gradually developed between the two sections. With every passing year came new arguments, each more bitter, more violent than the last.

Throughout these same years there also evolved two separate and conflicting theories as to the powers and rights of the Federal government versus the State governments. The contention of the Southern leaders was that, since the States had voluntarily entered the Union, they had an equal right to secede from the Union. The Federal government's power to dictate to a sovereign State was, therefore, limited. A citizen's allegiance must be first to his State, next to the Union.

Northern leaders asserted that the Federal government must be supreme or the laws of Congress would be worth no more than the paper they were printed on. No State could, at any time it pleased, declare a federal law to be null and void. A central government whose laws could be ignored was no government at all.

When Abraham Lincoln, the candidate of the new Republican Party, was elected President in November, 1860, the people of the South believed that the time had finally come to act. Characteristically, South Carolina, which had been threatening to secede for several years, led the way. Its ordinance of secession was passed on December 20, 1860. For a time, no other State followed, nor did the administration in Washington take any positive action. President Buchanan tried to evade the issue. Apparently all he wanted to do was to ride out the storm until the following March when he could drop the whole problem in President Lincoln's lap on Inauguration Day.

Of course, it was impossible to avoid the issue, to be blind to the problem. Having asserted the right to secede, South Carolina next claimed its right as a sovereign State to occupy the U.S. forts guarding the harbor of Charleston. These consisted of three small forts and one larger one, Fort Sumter, on an island at the entrance to the harbor. The Union garrison was so small (less than one hundred men) that it could not adequately defend any of these, but Major Robert Anderson did what he could. On the night of December 26, under cover of darkness, he concentrated his small force at Fort Sumter.

The authorities at Charleston were furious. They claimed that Major Anderson, by preparing to defend himself, had committed an act of war. The administration at Washington refused to order the garrison to surrender. A belief that the North was adopting a threatening policy swept through the deep South. We can best understand how rapidly this feeling spread by noting the dates on which these States seceded: Mississippi (January 9), Florida (January 10), Alabama (January 11), Georgia (January 19), Louisiana (January 26), and Texas (February 1). Representatives met at Montgomery, Alabama, and organized a provisional government. Jefferson Davis was chosen President of the Confederate States of America. With only two important exceptions, all of the U.S. forts and other public property were then promptly surrendered to the new government. These two were Fort Sumter, whose history we shall trace, and Fort Pickens in the harbor of Pensacola, Florida, which never did surrender.

On March 4, 1861, Abraham Lincoln was inaugurated as President. His inaugural address clearly stated his position but, of course, neither satisfied the Northern extremists nor appeased the South. He firmly informed the whole country that secession was unlawful. He promised to execute the laws of the Union in all the States and "to hold, occupy, and possess the property and places belonging to the Government." Southern leaders immediately interpreted this to mean that Fort Sumter and Fort Pickens were to be reinforced and all surrendered forts were to be recaptured.

This declaration sounds firm enough to have satisfied any Northerner but, near the end of his speech, the new President promised not to attack the people of the South, saying, "You can have no conflict without being yourself the aggressor." Many of the Northern people objected to this promise but, in spite of it, the Confederate Congress three days later passed an Army Act, authorizing the enlistment of 100,000 men for a year's service. Brigadier General P. G. T. Beauregard hastened his preparations for attack on Fort Sumter. Rumors and counterrumors filled the air.

Meanwhile, the supply situation at Fort Sumter was becoming acute. Both sides knew that the little garrison was running out of food. A relief expedition was organized to supply the fort with provisions only. President Lincoln notified the Governor of South Carolina that the attempt would be made. The Confederate government ordered General Beauregard to summon the fort to surrender. The summons was refused. It was repeated and again refused. A formal warning was then handed to Major Anderson that fire would be opened in an hour.

Wars started differently in those days!

For over two hours the fort was bombarded before the Union garrison began to fire in return. Not only was Fort Sumter so shorthanded that only a few of the guns could be manned, but there was also a critical shortage of powder bags. The shelling continued throughout the day. At nightfall, Fort Sumter ceased fire, but the Confederate batteries fired at intervals throughout the night. The next morning the artillery duel became more intense. At last the barracks were set afire by red-hot shot. The fire could not be subdued; it crept toward the powder magazine, the door of which was closed just in time.

By early afternoon the situation inside the fort was impossible. Major Anderson was forced to surrender.

Compare what happened the next day with a surrender in what we choose to call more modern times. On Sunday afternoon, April 14, with the permission of the Confederates, Major Anderson fired a fifty-gun salute to the U.S. flag and marched his troops, with colors flying and drums beating, aboard a waiting transport to return North. The victorious Confederates stood watching, with their hats off, in silent tribute to the valiant garrison.

In both the North and the South, events moved with increasing urgency. President Lincoln called for 75,000 volunteers for three months. All of the Northern States responded enthusiastically. Virginia, Arkansas, North Carolina, and Tennessee promptly seceded. In the border States, both sides had supporters and furnished recruits to both armies but no other States seceded. On the other hand, West Virginia broke away from Virginia and was later admitted as a Northern State.

As both sides prepare for the opening battles of the Civil War it would be well to compare their relative strengths. The total population of the twenty-two Union States was about twenty-two and a half million. The population of the eleven Southern States was about nine million, of which five and a half million were white, three and a half million were colored. Since the South did not employ colored troops, the odds would appear to be about four to one in favor of the North. In actual fact the odds were only about three to one because there was a very large peace party in the North which opposed the war and was a real thorn in the side of the administation. The people in the South were almost solidly in favor of the war.

Heavily outnumbered, the Confederate government made up some of the difference by much better management. President Davis, a West Point graduate, gave high command only to trained soldiers, former Regular Army officers receiving the highest positions, others being promoted as they proved their ability. Conscription was adopted early. Units were kept up to strength as much as possible, using a system of replacements similar to that in use in our army today.

On the other hand, many of the Northern generals at the beginning of the war were political appointees with little or no military experience. Also the Union government first attempted to fight the war solely with volunteers. In May, 1861, the term of enlistment was extended from three months to three years, but conscription was not adopted until 1863. As a result, the Union army did not reach its greatest effective strength until almost two years after the South. Another very curious mistake which never was corrected was the habit of continually forming new regiments of recruits, while the veteran regiments were allowed to fight battle after battle. As a result, the units with the most experience continuously lost men by death and wounds, exhausting themselves but receiving no replacements. Because of this fundamental difference between the armies we can never compare numbers in a battle by simply counting the regiments or brigades on each side.

As we all know, many of the officers of the Regular Army fought for the Southern cause. What happened to the enlisted men? Almost without exception, they stayed in the service, only three per cent deserting to the South. Surely then, the fact that the North had the soldiers of the regular service on its side should have counted heavily in its favor. It is true that wherever these units appeared on the field of battle they fought splendidly—but there were so few of them that the effect of their presence was negligible. The Regular Army amunted to only 16,000 men. They were scattered throughout the country; most were stationed on the Indian frontier, from which they could not be withdrawn with safety. The United States, as throughout most of its history, was completely unprepared for war.

The Regular Navy was even smaller than the Regular Army. It consisted of only six frigates, five sloops, and a few sailing vessels and gunboats. Fortunately, it was not preparing to fight a first-rate sea power, but a new country with no navy at all. One of President Lincoln's first actions, after the fall of Fort Sumter, was to declare a naval blockade of all the Southern ports. At first this was not effective since the U.S. Navy was so very small in size. Yet, small as it was, it was always larger than anything the South could produce. The Confederate States tried hard to establish a navy, but the North never let it grow. Gradually the Northern naval blockade became more and more effective until at last it was a stranglehold, and completely closed all Southern ports.

In addition to its superiority in manpower and in sea power, the North enjoyed another advantage which proved in the long run to be extremely important. Most of the heavy industries were concentrated in the Northern States. This is the type of advantage that is never immediately apparent unless a country has been preparing for war. It takes time to manufacture war materials. If, however, a war lasts long enough and, if industrial interests wholeheartedly swing into war production, this type of advantage may in the long run prove decisive.

It would appear that the North had all of the advantages, but this was not entirely true. One distinct advantage that the South had throughout the war was that of usually fighting on her own soil. Not only did this mean that her soldiers knew the country better, it also meant that the civilian population was friendly, ready to assist with information, shelter, and aid. Obviously this was very helpful to the Confederate armies; the effect upon the Union armies was also extremely important, though not so readily apparent. When Northern troops entered hostile territory it was not simply a question of marching to the battlefield. Guards had to be stationed all along the route to protect lines of communication, thus reducing the combat strength. The farther the army marched, the weaker it became. The defeat of a determined enemy on his own soil is never simple, the cost is always great.

Therein lay the other advantage of the Southern States, for they were not trying to conquer the North. What the Confederacy wanted was to be permitted to exist as a separate nation. When the South stood unconquered, winning great battles, particularly in the East, who could have said when the North might call it quits, and agree to an honorable peace? Who, at any time, from 1861 to 1863, could have simply enumerated the advantages and disadvantages of each side and surely predicted the outcome? The Northern peace party was always strong, continually asking if it was worth it to try to beat the South into submission. Such a vast territory it was to conquer; the North was itself invaded at times; the cost was so great: these were the insinuating arguments of the peace party in the North. These, and the hope of intervention by a foreign power, were the basis of the Southern hopes which ran so high in the first part of the war and never quite died until the last.

From Fort Sumter
to First Manassas

WHEN the State of Virginia seceded from the Union the North suddenly awoke to the fact that Washington, D.C., its capital, was in the front lines. If Maryland decided to secede, the city of Washington would be completely surrounded. There were only a few troops in the capital—and in Maryland there was a very strong feeling in favor of secession. Was history going to repeat itself? In the war of 1812 the enemy had captured Washington; it looked very much as if it would happen again.

Northern troops were hurriedly rushed to the scene. En route the Sixth Massachusetts Infantry was attacked by a mob in Baltimore. To prevent other troops from going through the city, the mayor of Baltimore ordered the railroad bridges to Washington destroyed. Then the telegraph wires were cut. The capital was completely isolated.

For six days no other units appeared. Finally, on April 25, the Seventh New York and the Eighth Massachusetts arrived. To reach the capital they had been forced to go by water, to land at Annapolis, then proceed to Washington, rebuilding the railroad as they went. Upon their arrival the telegraph lines were repaired and the North reassured. Baltimore was then occupied in force and Maryland coerced to remain in the Union.

At the same time that the North was making its capital secure against attack, it lost the services of an officer who might have become the new commanding general of all the Union armies. In 1861 the commander was General Winfield Scott, the hero of the Mexican War, but he was too old for active duty. Realizing that he could not lead the armies in the field he unofficially offered the command to Colonel Robert E. Lee, whom he considered to be the best officer in the Service. Unfortunately for the North, the offer was respectfully declined. According to General Scott the loss of this one officer was more costly than the loss of 50,000 veterans.

The State of Virginia promptly offered the command of its military and naval forces to Robert E. Lee. Obviously both sides knew the worth of this man. Under his direction the State began to prepare for war. Later, in June, when the Confederate War Department assumed control of operations in Virginia, Lee became the principal military advisor to President Jefferson Davis.

On April 27, four days after Lee accepted command of the Virginia forces, another figure appeared on the scene. A comparatively unknown colonel, Thomas J. Jackson, was assigned to command at Harper's Ferry. What a shock his arrival must have been to the soldiers! Until then they had been officered by a variety of generals sporting a tremendous amount of gold braid. Their new commander indulged in no fuss and feathers at all. His first action was to carry out his orders from the State Legislature to reduce all officers above the rank of captain. We can readily imagine what an uproar this caused among the recruits, who had been in the habit of electing their officers. After order was restored Colonel Jackson set to work to drill, discipline, and administer his new command.

Hurried training of recruits was the order of the day throughout the North and the South, although in no other place was it being done as efficiently and thoroughly as at Harper's Ferry. Everyone knew that raw troops had to be trained, but only a very few knew how to go about it, or even how much training was necessary. A typical case, especially in the North where there were so many political appointees, would be that of a regiment whose officers had no military experience trying to teach themselves and their soldiers this profession that none of them knew. The few regulars were spread too thinly; there was too much to do at once.

Worse still, military experience was often ignored in Washington either through neglect or ignorance. A citizen of

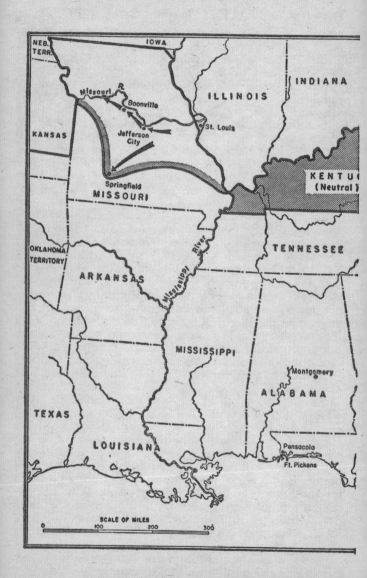

FROM FORT SUMTER
TO FIRST MANASSAS

Galena, Illinois, wrote to the Adjutant General to tender his services, saying that he thought himself competent to command a regiment if the President saw fit to appoint him. He meanwhile was helping train a company of infantry in his home town. This letter was lost in the files, not to be discovered until after the war. And so we find Ulysses S. Grant, the future commanding general of the United States Army, waiting patiently for an answer that never came, doing what he could to help others prepare for the coming stuggle. All about him commissions were being handed out, right and left, to anyone who had enough influence, or would recruit a unit and get himself elected to command. Nearly two months passed before the Governor of Illinois offered Grant a commission; this he immediately accepted, since he had received no reply from Washington.

Before we trace the history of any of the leaders of the war it would be profitable to clarify the boundaries of the North and the South. Due to the varying sentiments of the population of the border States it is manifestly impossible to draw an exact line between the two sides at the beginning of the Civil War. No matter where this line is drawn, there were Union volunteers south of it, Confederate volunteers north of it. It is practicable, however, to mark a line which will include the Union training camps on the Northern side, and those of the Confederates, such as Jackson's at Harper's Ferry, on the Southern side. At the same time this boundary will also serve to indicate the regions from which each made forward movements in the early months of the war.

Placing Maryland on the northern side of the line and Virginia on the south, we come next to Kentucky which at this period was maintaining a precarious neutrality. In Missouri the Union forces were primarily concentrated in St. Louis although the whole State was divided in its allegiance. Kansas, on the other hand, was strongly in favor of the Union except along its southern border.

With the two sides aligned generally in their starting positions we can now outline the major events that occurred between the fall of Fort Sumter and the First Battle of Manassas (Bull Run). On May 24 Union troops crossed the Potomac River into Virginia and seized Alexandria and Arlington Heights. To protect their bridgehead they built three forts, the first of the ring of forts that eventually encircled

Washington. Fort Corcoran was in Rosslyn, just across the Potomac via the present Key Bridge. Fort Runyon was just across the railroad bridge on the Virginia shore beside U.S. highway 1. The third one, Fort Ellsworth, was in Alexandria; the George Washington Masonic Memorial stands just a quarter of a mile to the east.

On June 10 there was a small engagement, won by the Confederates, at Big Bethel near Fort Monroe. Neither side, however, was yet ready to risk a battle in this, the main theater of war. Until mid-July all of the important fighting was to take place in either Missouri or West Virginia.

The governor of Missouri sided with the South and did his best to make the State secede. He was opposed by Francis P. Blair, a member of Congress, and an Army captain named Nathaniel Lyon. Together they organized and armed the Home Guards for the Union cause. During the month of May they secured the area around St. Louis. In June, Lyon, now a brigadier general, marched to Jefferson City and on June 17 attacked and defeated the Confederate forces at Boonville. It was only a small battle but had far-reaching results. It secured for the North, for all practical purposes, the capital of Missouri and the line of the Missouri River Valley. General Lyon immediately followed up his success by advancing southward to Springfield.

As noted previously, West Virginia broke away from Virginia and later became a new, separate State. In these mountainous, western counties of Virginia, sentiment was strongly in favor of the Union. When Northern forces, based on the Ohio River, moved into this friendly territory they were met with acclaim. The Confederates at Harper's Ferry, now under the command of Brigadier General Joseph E. Johnston, hastily evacuated their exposed position. (To keep the record straight, the number of troops stationed here had been increased and a general officer assigned to command. The former commander, Colonel Jackson, was serving as a brigade commander in Johnston's army.)

On the same day that Johnston evacuated Harper's Ferry (June 15) the South sent a small force into West Virginia to retain as much of the State as possible. These troops were defeated at the Battles of Rich Mountain on July 11 and Carrick's Ford on July 13 by greatly superior forces under the command of Major General George B. McClellan. These two battles won most of the State of West Virginia for the Union; they also gained for the victor an undeserved fame as another Napoleon. He awarded himself all the newspaper credit for operations in which his subordinates played the primary roles. The North was later to regret exceedingly the confidence they placed in him as a result of these two small battles.

There is one other event that also occurred in West Virginia early in the month of July that should be recorded here, not because it was significant, but simply to place the opposing forces in their proper positions for the opening of the First Manassas Campaign. On July 2, Union troops under a Major General Patterson forded the Potomac. They were met by a small reconnaissance force under Colonel Jackson at Falling Waters. A short engagement ensued in which a young lieutenant colonel of Confederate cavalry, J. E. B. Stuart, distinguished himself. The following day Patterson occupied Martinsburg where his troops remained until the opening of the campaign in which he was to play such an uneventful part. On this same day Colonel Jackson received his commission as brigadier general.

The First Manassas Campaign

FROM the moment that Richmond became the capital of the Confederacy it was obvious that a major battle must be fought in Virginia. The Union forces, gathered initially to protect Washington, gradually grew in strength until this became their main camp. Facing it, at Manassas, was the main camp of the Confederacy. The field commanders were two West Point classmates; Brigadier General Irwin McDowell of the Union army, and General P. G. T. Beauregard, the Southern hero of Fort Sumter.

By July the Union army around Washington numbered about 50,000 men. Beauregard's force at Manassas was approximately 20,000. About 3000 more were stationed at Acquia Creek, about thirty miles to the southeast. There was also a small detachment at Leesburg.

Patterson's army at Martinsburg, West Virginia, numbered about 18,000. Facing it was General Joseph E. Johnston's army of 11,000 men.

Almost three months had passed since President Lincoln had issued his first call for 75,000 volunteers; the people were becoming impatient. The terms of enlistment of these men were about to expire and most of them had not even seen a Confederate soldier. The cry of "On To Richmond" thundered daily in the newspapers. The generals said that the troops were not yet trained. They were correct, of course, especially in their estimate of the three-months men, whom they said could not be trusted. The administration in Washington felt impelled, however, to order an advance.

The Union plan of campaign was that McDowell would

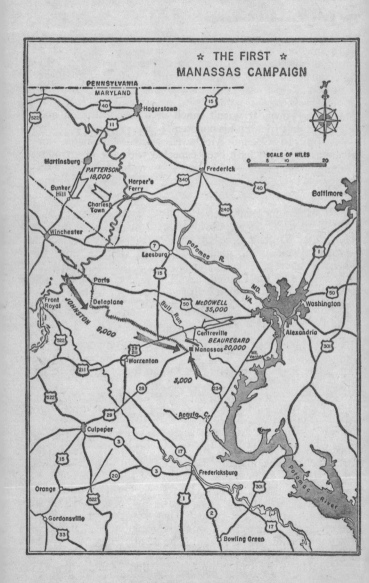

march with 35,000 men to Manassas and there attack Beauregard's smaller force. Patterson at Martinsburg was to keep Johnston from moving to Beauregard's assistance. On July 15 Patterson left Martinsburg and advanced to the little village of Bunker Hill which is just north of the Virginia border on U.S. highway 11. There he stayed for a day, then withdrew to Charles Town. It wasn't much of a demonstration and certainly didn't frighten his opponent.

On July 16 General McDowell started his march for Manassas. As could have been expected with any new troops marching together in such large numbers for the first time in their lives, the march was confused. The men were continuously harassed by constant stopping and starting. Then, as now, the main road was along U.S. highway 29. The distance from Washington is only about twenty miles, yet it took two and a half days to reach Centreville.

When McDowell started, Beauregard called for help. The Confederate forces at Acquia Creek and Winchester were ordered to his assistance. His own troops he moved into position along Bull Run. If reinforcements could arrive in time his army would be almost as strong as the Union army. With the troops at Acquia Creek it was only a question of marching time, moving north along the present U.S. highway 1, then cutting across to Manassas.

At Winchester, however, the problem was more complex. Johnston must slip away without letting the Union army know. If Patterson's forces also came to Manassas the Confederate armies would be heavily outnumbered on the battlefield. But Joseph E. Johnston was one of the outstanding generals of the war and he had an admirable cavalry commander who was also to make a name for himself. On July 18, leaving his sick men with a small guard, Johnston marched with 9,000 men toward Manassas. The cavalry, under Colonel J. E. B. Stuart, screened the movement so well that Patterson did not learn of it for two days.

As the leading brigade of Johnston's army marched toward Manassas, time was all-important, but the Confederates had their marching troubles too. When the first brigade halted at the village of Paris at 2:00 a.m. the troops were so exhausted that the brigade commander, General Jackson, stood guard himself, alone, so that his men could rest. A few months later they would have thought nothing of such a march, yet this was probably the best trained brigade in either army at that time.

At dawn Jackson awakened his men and resumed the march. Turning southward they reached Delaplane (formerly Piedmont), where they entrained for Manassas, arriving in the afternoon. If McDowell had acted promptly upon reaching Centreville this would have been the only additional Confederate brigade to reach the field. The bulk of Johnston's army did not arrive until the next day and one brigade did not arrive until the battle had begun.

There had been a small skirmish on July 18. McDowell had sent a portion of his force toward Manassas, but with orders not to bring on an engagement. Where the present State highway 28 crosses Bull Run a Confederate brigade from Virginia under the command of Brigadier General James Longstreet drove this force back in confusion. This small engagement elated the Southern forces and immoderately depressed a number of the Union soldiers. Some of the three-months volunteers whose enlistments had expired simply marched away from the battlefield, in spite of the earnest pleas of the Secretary of War who was paying a visit of encouragement to the army.

McDowell spent the next two days in reconnoitering the enemy position, organizing his troops, and bringing up supplies. July 19 and July 20 were simply lost to the Union army, while Confederate reinforcements from Acquia Creek, Winchester, and even a few from Richmond managed to reach the battlefield.

The First Battle of Manassas

MANY of the battles of the Civil War or the War Between The States, as it is often called in the South, have two names. This first big battle is an example. Southern leaders usually chose the name of the nearest town (Manassas), while Northern leaders often chose the name of a nearby stream or creek (Bull Run).

The fact that there are two names for this first battle of the war is perhaps appropriate since it leads to a certain amount of mild confusion, and at this battle there were many confusing factors. When two armies, each with only three months of training, meet in their first battle the number of mistakes and misunderstandings will be legion. We should not be surprised that the commanders' plans and orders were not executed with precision. We should rather expect troops to be slow in marching, staff officers to make mistakes, orders to miscarry. These things happen in the very best of armies.

At the First Battle of Manassas there was another factor that led to vast confusion. The soldiers were locally trained according to each commander's personal ideas, and sometimes they were also so uniformed and equipped. Some of the Union soldiers wore gray uniforms, some of the Confederates wore blue. From New York City came a regiment of Highlanders in kilts. The fez and baggy trousers worn by some of the North African soldiers of the French army appeared on the scene.

Even the flags in this battle were not helpful. The official Confederate Stars and Bars with a blue field and three stripes looked too much like the Union flag from a distance, especially if there was no breeze and it hung limply. At a critical period in the battle, when a new brigade appeared on the field, no one knew until the last moment whether it was Northern or Southern.

Is it any wonder that sometimes in this battle Union troops shot Northern soldiers, that the Confederates fired into Southern ranks?

Two results of this battle were that the Confederates adopted a new battle flag, the one best known today, and both sides hastened to adopt uniforms of a distinctive color, the Union blue and the Confederate gray.

The battlefield area near Bull Run is somewhat deceptive. At first glance it appears to be gently rolling country with a few hills, farms, and woods. There does not seem to be anything that would present a real obstacle to the movement of an army. But, on closer inspection, we find that the whole area is cut apart by streams running in narrow valleys between the hills. Of these, Bull Run is, of course, the largest. It presents a fairly formidable obstacle, if well defended. On close inspection of the ground, we can sympathize with General McDowell's delay, on July 19 and 20, in the hope of avoiding this obstacle. We can understand why he was slow to attack. But it does not alter the fact that the loss of these two days brought many additional Confederate soldiers to the field.

The morning of July 21, 1861, dawned bright and clear. The day promised to be hot. By an odd coincidence both armies prepared to launch an attack; each planned to assault the enemy's left flank. The senior Confederate officer on the field was General Johnston. He had just arrived from Winchester, he had never been to Bull Run previously, and there was not enough time for him to study the ground. The Confederate plan of attack was actually prepared by General Beauregard, who also issued the orders to execute it. These were confused and vague, some of them never reached his brigade commanders at all. Of the four brigades in the front line on the Confederate right, only those of Longstreet and Jones actually crossed Bull Run; Bonham's and Ewell's brigades were left waiting for orders. The Confederate attack plan was canceled when the Union army made its attack at the other end of the battlefield.

The Union plan for enveloping the Confederate left flank called for two crossings of Bull Run. The main attack led by General McDowell himself was to cross at 7:00 a.m., far beyond the Confederate left, near Sudley Church. The secondary attack was to be made at daybreak down the Warrenton Turnpike, straight toward the Stone Bridge. Although partially destroyed during the war, this bridge was later rebuilt and still stands, right beside the present U.S. highway 29. It is one of the principal landmarks of this battle and also of Second Manassas. It can be easily identified by the triangular monument in the center. It was here that the battle opened at 5:15 a.m. with a demonstration by the Union 1st Division.

It was soon obvious to Colonel Evans commanding the Confederate troops at the Stone Bridge that this was not the main effort. He had with him only a few troops which could easily have been pushed aside by the Union 1st Division, yet they made no real effort to do so. For almost four hours a slow cannonading continued. The only result of this demonstration was that the two Confederate brigades of General Bee and Colonel Bartow were ordered at 7:00 a.m. to march toward the Stone Bridge. General Jackson was sent with his brigade to a position of readiness nearby. This was the time set for the Union main attack to cross near Sudley Church—but it was two hours behind schedule. The Union plan of attack was an excellent one, except in the timing. The demonstration at the Stone Bridge served only to attract to the scene those Confederate troops which were to play so eventful a part in this battle. If the demonstration at the Stone Bridge had been timed to coincide with the main attack, or even to follow it, the Union plan would have had a better chance of success.

About 9:00 a.m. the Confederates were warned of the forces crossing near Sudley Church. The Union main attack had been observed from a high hill behind the Confederate lines. The warning message sent by flag signal, "wigwag," was probably the first use of this type of signaling in any war. It certainly produced fast action on the part of Colonel Evans. Leaving a guard at the Stone Bridge, he moved his small command rapidly to the left and rear, posting it on a hill north of the Warrenton Turnpike (U.S. 29), facing the enemy. Here he met the onslaught of the leading brigade of the Union 2nd Division led by Colonel A. E. Burnside.

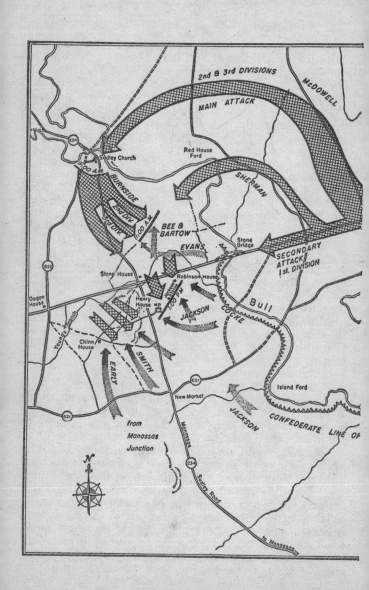

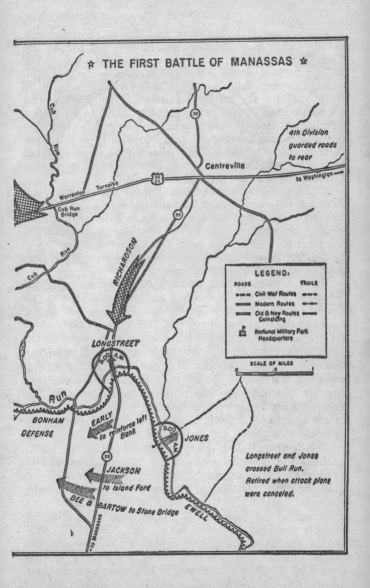

☆ THE FIRST BATTLE OF MANASSAS ☆

At this stage of the battle we find the main assault forces of the Union army, having rounded the Confederate left flank, facing a very small, but very stubborn, unit doing its best to hold until Confederate reserves could reach the scene. The other brigade of the Union 2nd Division entered the fray. Part of the 3rd Division joined in the attack, but so did some Confederate troops including the brigades of Bee and Bartow. Heavily outnumbered, the defenders clung desperately to their position. It began to look as if they were there to stay. The Union forces should have dispersed them long ago, but the attacks had been delivered piecemeal (regiment by regiment), straight to the front.

At this moment another Union brigade came on the field. Brigadier General William Tecumseh Sherman had found a crossing of Bull Run north of the Stone Bridge. His attack was not delivered straight to the front, but instead hit the Confederates on the right flank. The Confederate line broke. In his first major battle General Sherman was giving clear evidence of his ability as a tactician.

The Confederates fled across Young's Branch, past the Stone House (the best preserved and most conspicuous battlefield landmark) and across highway 29. They fled up the slopes of the Robinson House and Henry House Hills where the present-day Military Park Headquarters now stands. Desperately trying to rally the retreating forces, General Bee discovered a long, steady line of Confederate infantry waiting resolutely just behind the brow of the Henry House Hill. Another General, this time on the Confederate side, was demonstrating an unusual capacity for command. Marching to the sound of the firing, General Jackson had grasped the situation at a glance and formed his command in the best possible location to halt the enemy attack. His troops, whom he had worked so diligently to train, were standing firm awaiting the enemy attack.

It was here that General Bee, pointing to this brigade, shouted, "Look! There is Jackson standing like a stone wall! Rally behind the Virginians!" Though Bee, soon after, fell mortally wounded, his words did not die. "Stonewall" Jackson and the "Stonewall Brigade" will always live in the history of our country. The imposing statue of Stonewall Jackson erected by the State of Virginia in 1940 stands on the location where this dramatic incident occurred. The fleeing soldiers did turn and rally around the Virginians.

We now enter the second phase of the battle. It was in many ways a repetition of the first. The main assault forces of the Union army again faced a stubborn defense, formed this time around the strong core of Jackson's brigade. Again the Union army attacked. A mistake was made. Some of the artillery pushed too far forward. A swift cavalry charge led by Colonel J. E. B. Stuart, coupled with a counterattack by one of Jackson's regiments, and the guns were lost. The Union troops fell back, returned again to the attack. The front lines surged back and forth over the Henry House Hill.

Though both sides received reinforcements the greater Union strength began to tell. The Union line threatened to reach around the left of the Confederate line. At this critical moment the last of Johnston's brigades from Winchester, led by Brigadier General E. Kirby Smith, arrived on the scene. Hastily, it had detrained, formed, and marched to the battlefield. Attacking on the Confederate left, this brigade threatened the Union forces but it was not enough. More troops were needed. In the distance General Beauregard saw a column of marching men.

Was it Union or Confederate? Whichever it was it would surely win the day. Which flag was that at the head of the column? None could tell.

A breeze struck the colors, spread the flag—it was Confederate! Colonel Jubal A. Early's brigade, all the way from the opposite end of the battlefield, had come in the nick of time. All along the Confederate line, for the first time on any battlefield, rose the rebel yell as the men charged forward.

The Union line staggered backward, then collapsed. A few units retreated in good order. Many more simply walked away. Covered by the regulars and some units which had not been engaged, the retreating forces were comparatively safe from pursuit. The Confederates did not have enough troops available to make possible an assault on Washington. They did follow for a short distance and fired a few rounds of artillery at the road, upsetting a wagon, and temporarily blocking the way. This was what caused the panic, the oft-told hysterical flight of visiting Congressmen and their ladies, the society leaders who had come from Washington in their Sunday best to watch the battle. Many of the soldiers joined the mad rush. They never stopped until they reached Washington.

Of the 35,000 Union troops present during the battle only about 18,500 were actually engaged. They suffered about 2900 casualties, killed, wounded, captured, and missing. The Confederates had 32,000 present; approximately 18,000 of these eventually entered the battle but the bulk of the fighting was done by only a portion of this number. The Confederates suffered about 2000 casualties but also captured numerous guns, rifles, and other supplies and equipment abandoned in the flight to Washington.

From First Manassas to Shiloh

IMMEDIATELY after the stunning Union defeat at the First Battle of Manassas, President Lincoln called Major General McClellan from his victories in West Virginia to take command of the Union armies around Washington. Three months later, when General Winfield Scott retired, McClellan was placed in command of all the Union armies in both the East and the West.

At first, it appeared as if President Lincoln had picked just the right man for the job. The most pressing problem of the day was to organize and train the masses of recruits who were continually pouring into Washington. General McClellan proved to be a genius at this sort of work. The Army of the Potomac, as it was now called, began to look like an army in fact as well as in name.

The only trouble was that, as the months passed, McClellan did not seem to want to use that army to fight. He let the Confederates establish positions within sight of the capital at Washington; there were skirmishes as close as Bailey's Cross Roads, only five miles south of the city. He did nothing when the Confederates erected batteries on the lower Potomac, practically closing all navigation on the river. The only battle in this part of Virginia occurred on October 21 at Ball's Bluff, two miles north of Leesburg, when a Union force attempted to cross the Potomac and was severely defeated. The North began to question their new general's fighting ability. To the Southern generals he was fast becoming a joke. In their correspondence they referred to him as "The Redoubtable McC.", or simply, "George."

We must turn to the West to find the first important land battles of this period. In passing we may note that the North further strengthened its hold on West Virginia. In late July Union forces entered Charleston and in September won another small battle at Carnifax Ferry.

In the western theater, after winning the battle of Boonville in June, General Lyon had pushed southward to Springfield, Missouri. There he waited for supplies, which did not arrive, while the Confederates assembled against him a force nearly double his strength. Overconfident, or perhaps desperate, General Lyon attacked and at the Battle of Wilson's Creek was defeated on August 10, 1861. He was killed and his army forced to retreat. Temporarily, the Union advance in the State of Missouri had been checked, not to be resumed until the next year.

The notion that Kentucky could remain neutral, a Switzerland completely surrounded by the war, was absurd. Her sons were already fighting on both sides. It was simply a question of time before either the North or the South would feel the necessity of trespassing on her soil. Neither government wanted to be accused of being the first, but on September 3, 1861, Major General Leonidas Polk of the Confederate Army took the bull by the horns by seizing Columbus, Ky., on the Mississippi River. "Bishop" Polk, as his soldiers often called him, was a West Point graduate who had resigned his commission to enter the Episcopal ministry; at the outbreak of war he was the Bishop of Louisiana. At the request of Jefferson Davis he had accepted a commission as a major general but had not resigned his position in the church, intending to return to the ministry as soon as the war was over.

Brigadier General U. S. Grant promptly countered by seizing Paducah. That did it. Both sides rushed in troops as fast as they could. The Governor of Kentucky declared for the South; most of the legislature declared for the North. The State was split wide open. The year ended though without either side attempting a major engagement.

Remember the Confederate battle flag was changed after the First Battle of Manassas? The battle flag we know today has thirteen stars, yet only eleven States officially seceded. The other two stars represented Kentucky and Missouri whose Governors were pro-Southern. Both of these States were voted into the Confederacy by the Richmond Congress, yet neither actually seceded. Thirteen had been a lucky number in the American Revolution; would it prove to be lucky for the Confederacy?

During this year, 1861, the South was beginning to discover that President Lincoln's "paper blockade," as they scornfully called it when he made his first announcement, might become a threat to the life of the Confederacy. Gradually more and more warships were collecting outside the main Confederate ports. Blockade runners were growing cautious. In addition, the Union navy, in conjunction with the army, now began to seize important points along the coast. Although no important battles had as yet been fought on the sea, the naval war was already beginning to be a very one-sided affair.

The year 1861 had dragged to a close. The very first day of the year 1862 found Major General Stonewall Jackson on the march. Through snow, hail, and sleet storms, his troops reached the Potomac, destroyed the railway and telegraph lines for many miles, and then seized Romney, West Virginia. In this rapid campaign he captured large quantities of military supplies and effectively cut off the Union troops in West Virginia from the rest of the East.

To General Jackson's horror, he suddenly received a direct order from the Confederate Secretary of War to have the forces he had stationed at Romney returned to Winchester. Like a good soldier, Jackson promptly complied, although it completely nullified all of the results of his campaign. What was worse, the orders had not gone through his superior officer, General Joseph E. Johnston; they had been engineered directly by the soldiers and the commander at Romney, who were unhappy about their new assignment.

Such meddling in the affairs of a command could not be ignored. If a commander in the field was to have his orders countermanded at any time, without regard for himself, his superior, or the tactical situation, the Southern war effort would certainly end in chaos. Stonewall Jackson resigned. Only through the efforts of General Johnston and the Governor of Virginia, who said the South could not afford to lose him, was he induced to remain in the service. Suffice it to say, this incident taught the Confederate authorities a much-needed lesson.

In this same month of January, a small battle took place

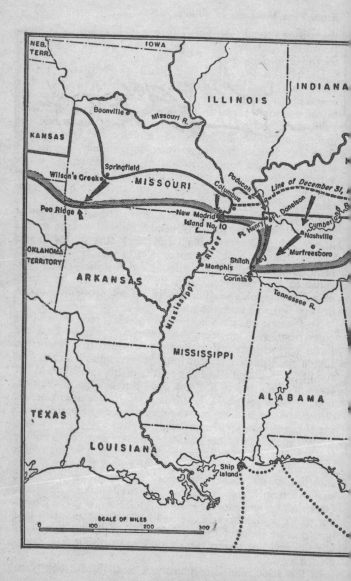

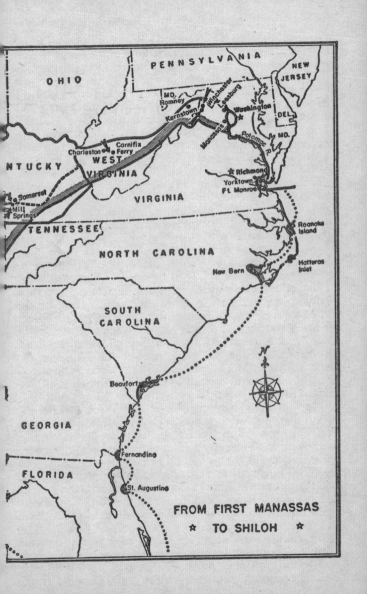

FROM FIRST MANASSAS
★ TO SHILOH ★

in eastern Kentucky. On January 19 Brigadier General George H. Thomas defeated a Confederate force at the Battle of Mill Springs, nine miles southwest of Somerset. In this battle, also called Logan's Cross Roads or Fishing Creek, only about 4000 soldiers were involved on each side, but it decided the fate of eastern Kentucky for nearly a year. It should have also answered any question concerning the loyalty of General Thomas, who was a native of Virginia. Oddly enough, however, some people in the North continued to eye him with suspicion up to the very close of the war, or at least until the Battle of Nashville in 1864.

The loss of eastern Kentucky was a blow to the South. It was similar to the loss of West Virginia. The Confederacy lost ground in each case, but in neither case was it decisive. There was little chance of a great invading army pouring across either of these mountainous regions. The roads were too poor, the supply problems too great. These losses could be considered as unfortunate events, perhaps to be recouped at a later date.

The next loss was an entirely different story. In western Kentucky we find three great natural avenues of approach: the Mississippi, the Tennessee, and the Cumberland Rivers. At the beginning of February a fleet of gunboats and troopships under command of Brigadier General Grant and Commodore Foote of the U.S. Navy sailed up the Tennessee. On the 6th, after a naval bombardment, Fort Henry surrendered. Most of the garrison escaped to Fort Donelson on the Cumberland River.

The Confederate commander in the West, General Albert Sidney Johnston, immediately sent reinforcements to Fort Donelson. With the rest of his army he hastened to vacate central Kentucky. It is unfortunate for the Southern cause that he did not go himself to take command at Donelson. The Confederates needed a leader there and they did not have one. Within a week, General Grant's army had marched overland and encircled the fort. Commodore Foote's gunboats, having sailed back down the Tennessee and then up the Cumberland, soon discovered, however, that this second fort was a tougher nut to crack. It not only did not fall after a naval bombardment but even inflicted serious damage on the Union gunboats. The garrison then attacked Grant's encircling lines and almost broke through. If the

Confederate commander, a Brigadier General Floyd, had been a more thorough, forceful leader the attempt might have succeeded.

With the failure of this one effort General Floyd decided that he, a former Secretary of War of the United States, could not afford to be captured. He escaped with a few of his troops on a steamboat.

The second-in-command, a general named Pillow, also abandoned his trust. He made his escape across the river on an old scow. This left Brigadier General S. B. Buckner to surrender the fort and its garrison.

At this point in the proceedings, we find a magnificent demonstration of what a real leader can do. There was, inside the fort, a Confederate colonel of cavalry who stated that he had not come to Fort Donelson "for the purpose of surrendering my command". He led his whole regiment out, plus some two hundred other men, through icy water up to the saddle skirts and lost not a single man. Colonel Nathan Bedford Forrest, one of the most outstanding cavalry leaders developed in this or any war, will be heard from again.

On February 16 General Buckner proposed the appointment of commissioners to discuss the terms of surrender. Grant's famous message, "No terms except unconditional and immediate surrender can be accepted. I propose to move immediately upon your works," quickly settled the issue. Approximately 11,500 men and forty guns were surrendered. Grant was immediately promoted to Major General.

The surrender of Fort Donelson was a terrific blow to the South. Already outnumbered in the West, the Confederacy could ill afford the loss of so many men. The whole line of defense across Kentucky gave way. General Albert Sidney Johnston was forced to retreat all the way to Murfreesboro, Tennessee. Union forces which had heretofore taken no part in the action advanced to occupy Nashville. Columbus on the Mississippi was abandoned; Union troops captured New Madrid and laid siege to Island No. 10. Almost simultaneously came word of another Confederate defeat at Pea Ridge (Elkhorn Tavern), Arkansas. The State of Kentucky appeared to be lost forever, and now the State of Missouri was firmly in the possession of the North.

Meanwhile, on the Atlantic coast, Union forces had occupied St. Augustine, Florida, seized Roanoke Island and

then New Bern, North Carolina. The famous battle between
the Monitor and the Merrimac had been fought. General
McClellan's army had finally moved, by water, to Fort Monroe and was standing in front of Yorktown. Union forces
were in Winchester; an important battle had been fought at
Kernstown. As we follow the campaign of Shiloh, we should
bear in mind that important events were taking place simultaneously in the East but since they culminated at a later
date we should follow the operations in the West first.

The Campaign of Shiloh

THE fall of Forts Henry and Donelson should have been the signal for a rapid, coordinated pursuit of a disorganized enemy. General Grant, whose command had been steadily reinforced until it now numbered 42,000, stood ready to advance. But he was only a district commander, subject to the orders of his department commander, Major General Henry W. Halleck. At nearby Nashville were 50,000 more Union soldiers, but they were in a different department, commanded by Brigadier General Buell. The over-all commander was still General McClellan in Washington.

Henry Halleck, known throughout the army as "Old Brains," because he had written a number of legal and military books, wanted to turn to the southwest and seize Memphis on the Mississippi. He always seemed to choose big cities as targets rather than the Confederate armies; perhaps he missed the point of some of his own books. On the other hand, Buell wanted to unite the two forces and advance due south. As for McClellan no one knew exactly what he wanted. There ensued a tremendous amount of letter writing while over 90,000 Union soldiers waited.

Meanwhile, although the Confederate forces were badly outnumbered, they at least had one man in sole charge of everything in the West. It is a curious fact that, until the appointment of Grant as a lieutenant general, we find no officer in the United States Army who attained a rank higher than that of major general. The Confederacy, however, recognized almost from the beginning the advisability of giving officers commissions appropriate to their commands. Short-

47

ly after the First Battle of Manassas, five full generals were appointed in the Confederate States Army: Samuel Cooper (the Adjutant General), Albert Sidney Johnston, Robert E. Lee, Joseph E. Johnston, and P. G. T. Beauregard. Confederate collar insignia, however, was confusing. You cannot tell a Confederate general's rank by looking at the old portraits; all general officers wore three stars regardless of rank.

The commander of all the Southern forces in the West was Albert Sidney Johnston. At the beginning of the war he had been probably the best known and most admired military figure in the South. An officer in the Regular Army, stationed in California, he had promptly resigned and started the long trek across the country. There was, of course, some doubt that he would arrive without being captured by either the Indians or the Union army. When he reached Richmond, the whole Confederacy had greeted him with acclaim. President Davis had promptly conferred upon him the important and immensely difficult job of command in the West. Now that he had lost Fort Donelson, his popularity had dropped to zero. The same Southern newspapers that had been praising him to the skies were now crying for his scalp. It seemed that the only real friend he had was President Davis, who firmly refused to relieve him from command.

Philosophically, Johnston set to work to repair the damage. He now had, as his second-in-command, General Beauregard of Fort Sumter and Manassas fame, recently transferred from the East. Together they strove to assemble their scattered forces. Corinth, Mississippi, was selected as the point of concentration. "Bishop" Polk, who had evacuated Columbus, was enroute with 10,000 men. General Johnston marched from Murfreesboro with about 15,000 more. New units were hastily organized; some 15,000 troops were gathered from as far away as the Gulf of Mexico. All of this took considerable time, but by the end of March the Confederate force near Corinth numbered something over 40,000 men.

Meanwhile General Halleck had ordered Grant's troops to advance south on the Tennessee River to make a reconnaissance. They were to destroy a few bridges and railroads, then return. They established themselves near Pittsburg Landing and stayed there awaiting developments. Grant, himself, did not join them for several days. He had been re-

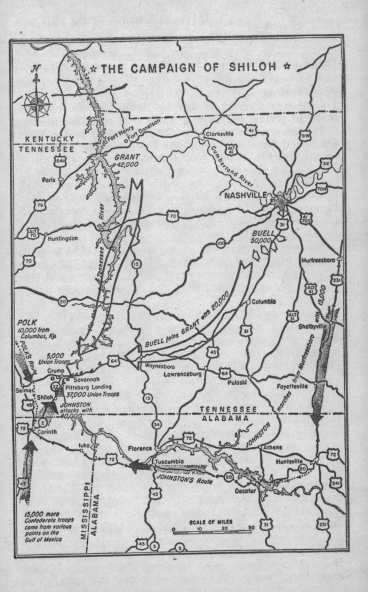

lieved from command by General Halleck, who had never even bothered to congratulate him on his victory at Fort Donelson, and who now had obtained permission from Mc-Clellan to place Grant under arrest. It is difficult to understand what really happened here. Halleck claimed that Grant had failed to reply to some official telegrams; Grant said he never received them. One story is that the telegraph operator was a Confederate spy who decamped with the whole file. There were other, somewhat complicated, factors involved, but one cannot help but wonder how much of all this was just plain jealousy on Halleck's part. Apparently he had never liked Grant, was overly ambitious himself, and found it difficult to watch his subordinate's success. Soon Halleck was forced to admit that he had no basis for preferring charges; he grudgingly restored Grant to his rightful command.

While all of this was taking place, President Lincoln changed the organization of the Union forces. McClellan was relieved as commander of all the Union armies and Halleck was placed in charge in the West. He soon ordered Buell's forces at Nashville to march to join Grant at Pittsburg Landing. Now it became a race against time—but only one side knew it. General Johnston saw quite clearly that he must strike Grant's army before Buell, now a major general, arrived on the scene. If Johnston could not strike in time, the Southern army would be hopelessly outnumbered. Gathering all the troops he could muster, Johnston marched northward from Corinth to Pittsburg Landing to attack.

The Confederate army started its march from Corinth on the afternoon of April 3. They were supposed to be in position to attack by early morning of April 5. With only about twenty miles to go, this seemed entirely feasible. But the troops were, for the most part, untrained in marching; there were only two dirt roads, through dense forests; a violent rainstorm turned the roads into pure mud; and the creeks overflowed, making marching at night almost impossible. The army did not get into position until late in the afternoon of April 5. The attack was postponed until early Sunday morning, April 6.

This delay of a day would not appear crucial, for although the Confederate army waited all that night only two miles from their enemy, the Union army did not learn of its presence. Grant had five divisions totaling about 37,000 around Pittsburg Landing, and one division of about 5000 at Crump six miles to the north. The troops were not entrenched nor disposed to receive attack. That day's delay was very important, however, for on that same day the leading division of Buell's army reached the opposite side of the Tennessee River about seven miles away.

There has been a great deal written about Grant's failure to entrench his positions at Shiloh. Undoubtedly, it would have been better to have dug trenches but we must remember that it was still early in the war. Even today the average recruit sees little point to digging unless someone is shooting at him; later on, these same soldiers would automatically dig without being told, whether they were expecting a fight or not. And they were not expecting to be attacked. Everyone from the top on down was concentrating on the drills which they all so sorely needed, for both armies were largely composed of men who had never heard a shot fired in anger.

Far more important than the failure to entrench was the Union neglect of adequate reconnaissance. It is extraordinary that the two armies stayed all night within two miles of each other and the Union army never knew it. Overconfidence after the success at Fort Donelson was probably the cause; no one seriously thought that the beaten Confederates would actually attack.

The Battle of Shiloh

AFTER the heavy rains which had proven so disastrous to the Confederate plan of attack, the day of battle, April 6, 1862, dawned bright and clear. On this beautiful Sunday morning most of the Union army was resting peacefully, unaware of the impending danger. There was one exception to this rule—in the Union division commanded by Brigadier General Prentiss. One of his brigade commanders, Colonel Everett Peabody, was suspicious of what might be hidden in those dark woods. At 3:00 a.m. he sent a small force forward to investigate. At dawn the first shots of the battle of Shiloh were fired by the Confederate outposts and Peabody's patrol.

This small action served to give some warning to the Union camps, but not enough. The charging Confederates burst upon Union soldiers only partially formed and partially ready. Breakfast was forgotten as the men dashed out to fight. General Prentiss managed to organize a hasty line a little in front of his camp. Brigadier General Sherman did not take time to move forward but lined up his division right in its camps. In the left center of his line was the old Shiloh Meeting House, or Church, from which the battle gets its name. Today there is a new church on this spot, erected in 1949; it is one of the principal landmarks of the battlefield. The commanders of the other Union division, acting on their own initiative, started their troops moving to the front. General Grant himself was not present at the time. He was across the Tennessee River, waiting for General Buell to arrive.

To make matters worse, the Union army found itself fighting in a three-sided box. On its right flank was a swampy stream, Owl Creek, which ran into Snake Creek, which in turn ran into the Tennessee River. On its left flank was another stream, Lick Creek, also running to the river in the Union army's rear. Through the only entrance to this box the Confederates poured in an irresistible avalanche. Driving from the southwest, General Johnston hoped to reach the river near Lick Creek, then swing northward, cutting off all escape or rescue by boat. Only a small portion of the Union army could then hope to get across the Owl and the Snake.

Obviously then, to follow the plan, the main Confederate effort should have been made near Lick Creek; there the bulk of the army should have been concentrated. For this battle, though, the Confederates adopted an unusual formation. Major General Hardee's Corps formed the first line; Major General Bragg's Corps formed behind it in a second parallel line. Major General Polk's Corps and the reserve corps commanded by Brigadier General Breckinridge (who a year and a half before, had run against Abraham Lincoln, as the Southern Democrats' nominee for the presidency) formed in rear. No one commander was responsible for any particular part of the line (right, left, or center).

The battlefield of Shiloh, now a pleasant park, was then densely wooded except for a few farms. Most of it was covered with thick underbrush and interlaced with winding ravines and country roads. Control of troops was extremly difficult. It was entirely impractical in the first stages of the attack to follow Johnston's plan. Every unit of the first two Confederate corps simply attacked straight to its front into Prentiss' and Sherman's troops.

The shock of this unexpected attack was too much for recruits to bear. For many of them this was their first battle. The whole left brigade of Sherman's Division dissolved in flight. About 9:00 a.m. Prentiss' Division broke and fell back to a new line. When Grant arrived on the field he found all five of his divisions engaged in a desperate struggle for survival. Already he had ordered the leading unit of Buell's army to move forward. Now he sent for Major General Lew Wallace's Division at Crump (six miles away). But could his army hold until these arrived?

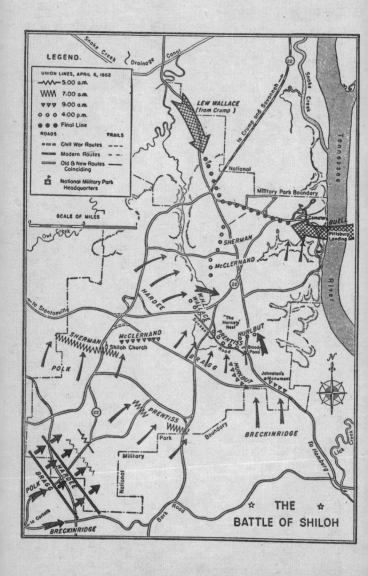

Everywhere the Confederates were pushing forward. The Union situation looked hopeless, but battles are seldom entirely onesided. In the center of the line was a naturally stong position, a dense woods with open fields on either side. Along this line ran an old sunken road which proved to be of immense defensive value. Here, where portions of the division of Generals Hurlbut and W. H. L. Wallace stood ready to resist attack, General Prentiss managed to rally some of his fleeing men. The victorious Confederates, surging forward, were brought to an abrupt halt when they reached the new line. This place has become known to history as "The Hornets' Nest" because of the stinging shot and shell that issued from it. Again and again, the Confederates charged. All efforts to take it by assault failed. Massed artillery fire failed to dislodge the defenders.

On the flanks, though, the Confederates were still faring well. Sherman and Major General McClernand, fighting stubbornly, were slowly forced back on the Union right, continuously outflanked from position to position. At the opposite end of the field the Union line was enveloped, but it was here at 2:30 p.m. that the Confederate commander, General Albert Sidney Johnston, was mortally wounded. He actually died from loss of blood. With modern medical care his wound probably would not have been fatal. The monument erected in his memory is another of the famous landmarks of the battle. Between Johnston's Monument and "The Hornets' Nest" is a well-known location called Bloody Pond. So many of the wounded from both sides came to this spot that the waters were said to have been stained red by their blood.

The Confederates never did break "The Hornets' Nest"; they eventually surrounded it, but not until late in the afternoon. Colonel Peabody and General W. H. L. Wallace were killed; General Prentiss with some 2200 men was forced to surrender. The loss of these troops was a serious blow to the Union army but they had, by their stubborn, last-ditch defense, enabled the remainder to form another line, still farther in the rear. Near the river a number of Union guns were hastily put into position to protect Pittsburg Landing. In a final desperate effort two brigades of Confederates, almost without ammunition, charged into the fire of this massed artillery. If their assault had succeeded, they would have carried out Johnston's original plan to cut off escape and rescue from across the river. The vanguard of Buell's forces arrived in time to help defeat this final effort.

Sunday, April 6, was definitely a Confederate victory but the gains they had won could not be realized. Grant's original forces had been reduced to about 7000 effectives, but during the evening and night, 25,000 fresh troops arrived to swell the Union ranks. Why it took so long for Lew Wallace and Buell to get there, and whose fault it was is still being argued, but by the next morning the Union army was definitely the stronger. The Confederates could only muster some 20,000 effective troops. We must remember that the Southerners were also essentially an army of recruits and there had been a great deal of straggling in their ranks.

On Monday, April 7, the tables were completely turned. General Grant attacked but it was not to be an easy Union victory. The Confederates, under General Beauregard, held their ground stubbornly for hours. In the early afternoon their line was still in front of Shiloh Church, where Beauregard had established headquarters. Finally, seeing that they had no chance of any victory, they withdrew from the field. There was no pursuit. The Union army was glad to see them go.

The casualties at Shiloh were a tremendous shock to both the North and the South. Each side lost about a quarter of the total troops engaged. The Confederates suffered about 10,700 killed, wounded, captured, and missing. The Union losses totaled over 13,000, of which by far the greater number came from Grant's command. By comparison, the casualties at the First Battle of Manassas faded almost into insignificance. Both the North and South awoke to the unpleasant fact that this was going to be a long and bloody war.

The Battle of Shiloh added nothing to the reputation of any general on either side—with one exception. General Grant had particularly noted the stubborn defense that General Sherman had made against overwhelming odds. From then on, Grant was to rely more and more heavily upon this man until, at the last, it was this team that was to bring the war to an end. As an immediate reward for his outstanding service Sherman was promoted to major general.

There was another officer present at Shiloh who was also to become famous, but not as a general. This was Lew Wallace, the future author of "Ben Hur."

From Shiloh to Antietam

APRIL 7, 1862, was a very black day for the Confederacy for it not only marked the second day at Shiloh but the surrender of Island No. 10 on the Mississippi. It fell to a combined land and naval force commanded by Major General Pope and Commodore Foote, the same officer who had been with Grant at Forts Henry and Donelson. From a military point of view, the most interesting development of this campaign was the attempt of two Union gunboats to run by the strong Confederate batteries under cover of darkness. Almost everyone on both sides expected the ships to be sunk, but both escaped with little damage.

A few days after the Battle of Shiloh there occurred one of the most daring exploits of the entire war. Led by a Union spy named James J. Andrews, some twenty soldiers from Ohio dressed in civilian clothes, slipped through the Confederate lines to as far south as Marietta, Georgia, where they boarded a northbound train as passengers. When the train crew stopped for breakfast, they stole the engine, together with three or four boxcars, and headed toward Chattanooga. The conductor of the train, Captain W. A. Fuller, together with two companions, started in pursuit—on foot. Soon they found a handcar, then an engine, but could not send messages ahead because the fleeing men cut the telegraph lines.

Unfortunately for the Union men, there were several unexpected delays. Also it had begun to rain so that their plan to burn the bridges behind them failed. Fuller finally managed to send a message ahead. Andrews and his men had to abandon their engine and run for the woods. Eventually they were all captured. Andrews and seven others were executed; the others escaped or were later exchanged.

Meanwhile at Shiloh, "Old Brains" Halleck had arrived to take command of the armies in the field. There he concentrated all his forces, including those of General Pope from Island No. 10, until he had an army of 120,000 men. Then very slowly and cautiously Halleck started toward Corinth, Mississippi. Every night he forced his men to stop and dig entrenchments. During the day they would move forward a mile or so, then stop to dig themselves into the ground for the night. Halleck's disgusted soldiers almost literally dug up the whole countryside from Shiloh to Corinth. It was not until the end of May that Halleck reached his objective. By the time they entered the city, Beauregard's army had moved.

We shall leave Halleck to his digging and review the situation in the East where important events had been occurring during the past three months. On March 9, 1862, at Hampton Roads off Norfolk, Virginia, one of the most important battles in the history of naval warfare had been fought. It was the duel between the _Monitor_ and the _Merrimac._ There steam-powered, ironclad men-of-war had met in combat for the first time. It was a drawn battle, but it started every nation of the world building completely different types of naval vessels. The day of the wooden warship was practically finished.

During this same month of March, 1862, the Union Army of the Potomac finally began its move toward Richmond. It did not take the overland route but was transferred by water to Fort Monroe, Virginia. From there it was to advance up the Peninsula, the neck of land between the James and York Rivers. At first glance, this end run, using the navy to save many miles of walking and fighting, might seem like a good plan. The distance from Fort Monroe to Richmond is considerably less than that between Washington and Richmond. Furthermore, the Union army thus avoided having to make a number of river crossings. From a strictly military point of view there were some advantages to this scheme.

There was, however, one important disadvantage that was completely ignored by the Union commander, Major Gener-

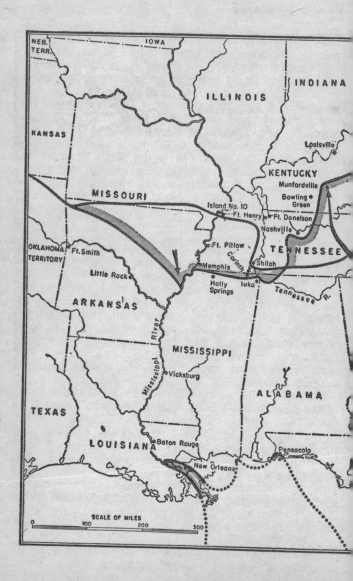

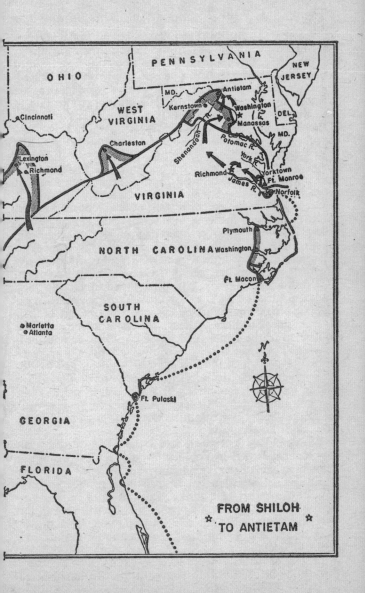

FROM SHILOH
TO ANTIETAM

al George B. McClellan. The prime objection to the plan was that President Lincoln was greatly concerned, and rightly so, for the safety of Washington. He had, from the first, doubted the wisdom of this end run and, therefore, required that a large number of troops be left behind to guard the capital. Almost anyone else would have paid the closest attention to the wishes of the President of the United States, but not George B. McClellan. Somewhere along the line he had acquired the idea that he, and he alone, could save the country. He thrived on fame and popularity, and he was popular with the soldiers. He loved to gallop by in front of the troops and listen to them cheer as he flourished his hat or saber.

So, in spite of the expressed views of the President, General McClellan started his move to the Peninsula. He planned to take 150,000 men. Other Union forces were to chase the Confederates out of the Shenandoah Valley, then move to Manassas as an additional protection for Washington. As we shall see when we get to Jackson's Valley Campaign, this part of the plan did not work. President Lincoln then discovered that he had been shortchanged by McClellan on the number of troops that he had prescribed be left behind. The President withheld General McDowell's Corps for the protection of the capital, and in addition took another division which had not yet embarked on the transports and sent it to West Virginia. By ignoring the President, and by disobeying his orders, McClellan had lost the services of a large part of his army before he had barely started. If he had taken the overland route, as General Grant was to do two years later, the greater part of these lost units would still have been under his command.

We should also note that, at this time, there was no military commander left in Washington to direct and coordinate the movements of the several armies in the field. As soon as McClellan left Washington he had been relieved as commander of all the Union armies. This was quite proper, since he could not be expected to command his own army in the field and all the other armies at the same time. It also indicates that he had, by this time, lost the complete confidence of the President.

In spite of the fact that McClellan did not have as large a force as he had planned, his army still heavily outnumbered the Confederates, and yet he spent a whole month in front of Yorktown. When he was almost ready to attack, the Confederates retreated. It took him another month to get near Richmond.

When General McClellan was finally forced to face a large enemy army his personality underwent a rapid change. His confidence disappeared. He flooded the mails to Washington with complaints and requests for reinforcements. He constantly magnified in his mind the numbers of the enemy. In those days, the intelligence system of an army was not well organized, so McClellan provided his own. He employed the Pinkerton Detective Agency to keep him informed of the movements and strength of the Confederates. These men were undoubtedly competent in their own profession, but of military matters they were wholly ignorant. Their reports, which McClellan trusted more than those of his subordinates, were invariably exaggerated. McClellan undoubtedly preferred to believe them because they coincided with his own fears. This was the man who now led the Union Army of the Potomac to Richmond.

It is strange that at the same time in both the East and the West we should find two large armies, both commanded by very cautious generals, simultaneously advancing at a snail's pace. We can temporarily leave both Halleck at Corinth and McClellan at Richmond and turn to a completely different part of the war where the action was moving rapidly.

We have seen how the Union forces were advancing down the Mississippi with the obvious intention of cutting the Confederacy in two. Now in late April of this year the navy struck at the lower Mississippi. A Union fleet, under the command of Admiral David G. Farragut, the most famous naval figure of the Civil War, captured New Orleans. During the next two months he twice went as far up the river as Vicksburg. The South began to be greatly worried about the defense of the remaining portion of the river still held by her forces.

During April and May of 1862 the future of the Confederacy looked very dark indeed. This picture was to change with dramatic suddenness. In the Seven Days Battle, McClellan was driven away from Richmond. In the month of August came the Second Battle of Manassas, another Confederate victory. By mid-September the Confederate Army of

Northern Virginia was invading Maryland. Concurrently a small force invaded West Virginia and recaptured Charleston.

In the West also the Confederates were on the march. General Halleck, after capturing Corinth, divided his huge army into several parts, thereby making it possible for the Confederates to resume the offensive. In July and August Confederate cavalry under Colonels Forrest and Morgan played havoc with the Union supply lines in middle Tennessee. In mid-August Major General Kirby Smith marched north and by the end of the month had won a victory at Richmond, Ky. General Bragg, who had replaced General Beauregard and was now the South's sixth full general, was also on his way toward Kentucky. Only in west Tennessee and along the Mississippi where Grant and Sherman were stationed and in Arkansas did the North appear to be holding anything of what it had gained at Shiloh. Gettysburg is usually referred to as "the high-water mark of the Confederacy" but the late summer of 1862 is the only period in the war when her armies were advancing victoriously in both the East and the West.

Jackson's Valley Campaign

MANY thousands of words have been written about Jackson's Valley Campaign. It has been studied very carefully in all its details, both here and abroad, as a model of its kind. Upon it rests a great part of Stonewall Jackson's reputation as a military genius.

The operations covered a period of three months from the middle of March to the middle of June, 1862. The forces involved marched up and down the Shenandoah Valley no less than five times, or a total of two and a half round trips. To attempt to trace on one map the movements of all the troops throughout this campaign would only result in confusion. In too many instances we would find the same soldiers retracing their own steps on the same roads. The present U.S. highway 11 corresponds very closely to the old Valley Turnpike which was the road most frequently used. The next most important route used is now state highway 12, which again corresponds very closely to the old route, except for a section in the middle, south of Luray and north of Elkton. During the Civil War this part of the road ran entirely east of the river.

Throughout this campaign the Confederates were heavily outnumbered, yet managed to win every battle but the first. But this is only one side of the story. The real importance of the campaign was the part it played in aiding the main Confederate army to save Richmond. To put it another way, Jackson's Valley Campaign prevented McClellan from receiving the reinforcements that might have enabled him to defeat the Confederate forces opposing him, capture Richmond, and win the Civil War by the summer of 1862.

To understand these operations it is imperative that we review the general situation in the East in this early spring. At Washington General McClellan was preparing an army of 150,000 men to take to the Peninsula. The Confederate Army of Northern Virginia opposing him, under General Joseph E. Johnston, numbered less than one third as many. At Winchester in the Shenandoah Valley, General Jackson had under his command about 4200 men. Facing him was a Union force under Major General Banks of over 20,000 and another army almost as large stood ready in nearby West Virginia.

The Union plan was for General Banks to chase Jackson's small force out of the Valley, then move east to Manassas to protect Washington. McClellan could then proceed to the Peninsula without any fears for the safety of the capital.

It is doubtful if anyone in the North thought very much, one way or the other, about the Confederate force at Winchester. At that time, Jackson's name meant little, although he had done exceedingly well at the First Battle of Manassas. Some people knew that he was a graduate of West Point who had served in the Mexican War and then resigned to teach mathematics at the Virginia Military Institute. Other knew that he was deeply religious; most of those who were close to him had learned that he was a very determined, studious individual, exacting and precise. His appearance was not striking. He dressed simply; in fact, he did not at all resemble the popular ideal of a handsomely uniformed military man. He was quiet, soft-spoken, seldom smiled, and never exhibited the slightest interest in pomp and ceremony. His soldiers had learned a few other things about him: that he was a stern disciplinarian; that he would march their legs off to get into a battle; that he always seemed to know exactly what he wanted; that he never confided in anyone. They were to learn a great deal more about him, and so were their enemies.

By early March of 1862, General Banks had crossed the Potomac. Jackson evacuated Winchester; Banks promptly occupied it. To simplify the somewhat complex maneuvers that followed, they have been divided into groups and each group lettered to correspond to the battles fought. The map has been lettered to conform.

A. The Battle of Kernstown (March 23, 1862)

The Union forces followed Jackson south along the Turnpike (U.S. 11) until they became convinced that he had fled from the Valley. General Banks then started his withdrawal toward Washington. This was exactly what Jackson was to prevent. His mission was to hold as many of the enemy in this region as he could, thus helping Johnston's main army. The more Union troops Jackson kept busy in the northwest, the fewer McClellan could take south to Richmond.

Although the Union forces remaining in the Valley still outnumbered his, Jackson marched hastily northward and struck Banks at Kernstown. After a prolonged struggle, the Confederates were defeated and driven from the field. Tactically it was a defeat, but let us see what happened from the over-all strategic point of view. First, General Banks could not believe that Jackson would have dared to attack unless he had been reinforced and had a large army at hand. Banks hastily recalled the troops he had sent to Washington. McClellan agreed to this change.

At this same time President Lincoln made the discovery that he had been shortchanged on the garrison to protect Washington. He kept McDowell's Corps from going to the Peninsula and also sent a division to West Virginia. How much of this decision by the President was McClellan's fault for disobeying orders, and how much of it was due to Jackson's attack at Kernstown we cannot say. In any case the result was that instead of fewer troops watching Jackson, the North was sending more against him. Although the battle was a Confederate defeat, it had produced a great strategic victory; McClellan's main army had been materially weakened.

B. The Battle of McDowell (May 8, 1862)

Again ordered to clear Jackson from the Valley, General Banks proceeded very slowly. It took him a month to reach Harrisonburg. At the same time Major General Fremont, the Union commander in West Virginia, sent some of his troops southward toward Staunton. Jackson then moved to a flank

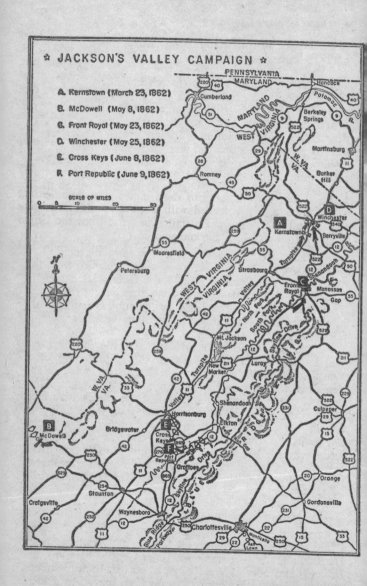

☆ JACKSON'S VALLEY CAMPAIGN ☆

A. Kernstown (March 23, 1862)
B. McDowell (May 8, 1862)
C. Front Royal (May 23, 1862)
D. Winchester (May 25, 1862)
E. Cross Keys (June 8, 1862)
F. Port Republic (June 9, 1862)

SCALE OF MILES
0   10   20   30

position in the Blue Ridge Mountains at Swift Run Gap where he received reinforcements (Major General R. S. Ewell's Division). Leaving part of his troops to threaten Banks, he marched with the rest as if he were going toward Richmond. Even his own men thought that was their destination. They were disappointed and heavyhearted at the thought of leaving their families and homes to the enemy. When they boarded the railroad trains they were certain they were leaving the Valley. But the trains started west, not east. They unloaded at Staunton to the great surprise and joy of the citizens who thought they had been deserted. Hastily the troops marched westward. Just short of the town of McDowell they were attacked by the Union forces. The fighting was very severe, but ended with Fremont's men retreating into West Virginia. Jackson started in pursuit but the Union forces set the woods on fire and escaped.

Meanwhile, back in Washington, President Lincoln had begun to realize that there were too many men being held idle there. He decided to let General McDowell's Corps go to Richmond. Banks was to send some of his troops too. Once again the Union forces stopped chasing Jackson and turned northward, sending a division out of the valley toward Washington.

C & D: *The Battles of Front Royal and Winchester (May 23-25, 1862)*

Although the Union troops remaining must have expected Jackson to take some action he completely surprised them. Instead of following the Valley Turnpike (U.S. 11), he turned off, marched to Luray, then attacked and overwhelmed a small garrison at Front Royal. Banks, who at first could not believe that Jackson's men could march that fast, fled to Winchester. There he tried to make a stand, was badly defeated, and fled across the Potomac. Jackson pursued all the way to the river, capturing a number of prisoners and large quantities of supplies.

The people in Washington became greatly alarmed for the safety of the capital. McDowell's movement to Richmond was immediately canceled; half of his whole corps was dispatched toward the Valley. The division under Major General Shields that Banks had sent toward Washington was turned around and started back. From West Virginia, General Fremont was also ordered immediately to the Valley. Fremont, marching east on the present-day state highway 55, was to join Shields marching west from Manassas Gap on the same road. The idea was to cut off Jackson before he could retreat from the Potomac. Jackson eluded them with comparative ease. Again, on a grander scale, he had ruined McClellan's hopes for reinforcements, attracting more troops then ever before toward the Valley, away from Richmond and Johnston's army.

E & F: The Battle of Cross Keys and Port Republic (June 8-9, 1862)

This time the Union forces pursued Jackson in two columns. They could not catch him until they reached the place where he chose to wait for them. On June 8, General Ewell's Division of Jackson's army held off Fremont's western column at Cross Keys. On the following day, Jackson severely defeated Shields' eastern column in the Battle of Port Republic. Both retreated northward. McDowell's orders to go to Richmond were again canceled. A few days later Jackson slipped away from the Valley to join Lee at the Seven Days Battle in front of Richmond. None of the Union troops that had fought against him ever did reach McClellan.

Another result of Jackson's Valley Campaign was the fame that became attached to his name and to his soldiers of the Valley. Because they marched so far and so fast they became known as Jackson's "foot-cavalry." The Union forces never knew when or where they might suddenly appear. At Kernstown and at Front Royal they had supposed Jackson to be miles away when he suddenly attacked their outposts. Yet, at the same time, Jackson seemed to always know just where his enemy was. A great deal of the credit for this must go to the Confederate cavalry. Born and bred to the saddle they were definitely superior to the Union cavalry. They also had an outstanding leader, Colonel Turner Ashby, who, under Jackson's guidance, did magnificent work. Unfortunately for the future of the Southern cause he was killed just before the end of this campaign.

To another officer in the Confederate army must go a great deal of the credit for the success of the campaign. General Robert E. Lee, acting as President Davis's military advisor, had also seen the possibilities inherent in such an operation. He was the one responsible for sending reinforcements to Jackson at a time when it seemed that every available man should be concentrated at Richmond.

In the final analysis, however, it was Stonewall Jackson's Campaign. Mention of others does not in the least detract from his responsibility for its outstanding success.

The Seven Days Battle

WE return now to General McClellan moving slowly toward Richmond with the Union Army of the Potomac. By the latter part of May they had approached to within six miles of the city. On May 31 the Confederates attacked a portion of the Union army. In this battle, known as Fair Oaks or Seven Pines, the Southern troops were repulsed. We can well imagine how this raised the morale of the Union soldiers and correspondingly disheartened the Confederates, who now found themselves on the losing end of a battle fought almost within the city limits of their capital. As if this were not enough, their commander, General Joseph E. Johnston, had been so severely wounded that there was some doubt that he would survive.

In this gloomy crisis, with Richmond apparently on the point of capture and the fate of the Confederacy hanging in the balance, Jefferson Davis turned to the man who had been acting as his chief military advisor. He thereby made the best appointment of his whole four years as President. On June 1, 1862, Robert E. Lee became the new commander of the Army of Northern Virginia. He immediately set his men to work to strengthen the defenses of Richmond. At the same time he hastened the plans and preparations for the arrival of reinforcements from Georgia and the Carolinas. His attack plans also involved bringing Jackson's force secretly from the Valley. All of this took time. Almost a month was to pass before General Lee was ready to fight a battle.

In the meanwhile there occurred a most unusual exploit, a raid completely around the Union army. This daring enterprise was conducted by Lee's cavalry commander, Brigadier General J. E. B. Stuart. Such an endeavor was typical of this man. A dashing cavalryman who dressed and acted the part, "Jeb" was the idol of his soldiers. During his West Point days he had acquired the nickname of "Beauty" Stuart, primarily because he was not handsome. Now, with a full dark beard, a plume for his hat, and a magnificent gray uniform with a flowing cape, "Jeb" was the hero of thousands of young men. According to tradition, wherever he went he was accompanied by a corporal named Sweeny, an expert on the banjo. General Stuart liked his music with him.

The raid around McClellan's army undoubtedly started off gaily enough, but before it was over it became a real race. Stuart and his men did considerable damage in the rear of the Union lines, but they were closely followed and crossed the James River just in front of their enemy. The Union cavalry commander whose troops pursued him so relentlessly was none other than Brigadier General Cooke, Stuart's own father-in-law.

Near the end of June, General Lee was ready to execute his carefully laid plan. A word or two concerning the topography of the country will aid greatly in understanding the several battles that followed. To the north and east of Richmond the terrain is flat or gently rolling. During the Civil War it was more extensively wooded than it is now, but the woods did not, even at that time, present any real problems. The major obstacles to movement were the swamps and marshes. From a military point of view the most important feature of the terrain is the Chickahominy River. This small stream winds its way through numerous marshy areas which are difficult to cross, especially in rainy weather. Between the Chickahominy and the James is White Oak Swamp, another difficult region. All of the roads east of Richmond were dirt roads—and it rains heavily in Virginia in the month of June. Today there is a good, all-weather road called the Battlefield Route (State Highway 156) which runs completely through the country fought over in the Seven Days Battle. It also passes through the battlefield area of Fair Oaks or Seven Pines.

In late June, 1862, General McClellan's army was split

into two parts by the Chickahominy. One corps was on the north bank; the other four were south of the river. McClellan has been severely, but perhaps unfairly, criticized for allowing his army to be thus divided. We must remember that he was still hoping that McDowell's Corps from Washington would arrive to reinforce his army. He therefore had to keep some troops north of the river to make contact with them when, and if, they arrived.

Lee decided to attack this isolated Union corps, commanded by Brigadier General Fitz-John Porter, simultaneously in front and on the flank. The frontal attack was to be made by Major General A. P. Hill's Division. Stonewall Jackson, coming secretly from the Valley, was to make the flank attack. Other troops were, of course, to follow and support the assault forces. The first day of the Seven Days was consumed in preparations for this attack. The second day did not go according to plan. For once in his life Stonewall Jackson was late. Hill waited until the middle of the afternoon then attacked across Beaverdam Creek and was severely repulsed. Porter's Union Crops then retired to a new position. This second day of the Seven Days (June 26) is also called the Battle of Mechanicsville.

On June 27 the Confederates again assaulted Porter in his new location. In this battle the Confederates outnumbered the Union forces two to one. The troops of A. P. Hill, Jackson, and eventually those under Major General James Longstreet were all employed. Although Porter's Corps received some reinforcements the Union line was broken, but darkness finished the fight, and the Union troops were able to escape across the Chickahominy. This third day is called the Battle of Gaines' Mill.

On the fourth day there was very little combat action but McClellan's army was intensely busy. All the Union supplies had come from a base on the York River several miles to the northeast. As a result of the previous two days fighting their food and ammunition were about to fall into Confederate hands.

The Seven Days Battle can be divided into two distinct phases. The first had consisted of the attack on Porter's Corps north of the Chickahominy and the cutting of the Union supply line. In the second phase McClellan's army was hastily

THE
SEVEN DAYS
☆ BATTLE ☆

━━━ Battlefield Route
State Highway 156

SCALE OF MILES
1 2 3 4 5

Mechanicsville – June 26, 1862
Gaines' Mill – June 27, 1862
Savage's Station – June 29, 1862
Glendale (or Frayser's Farm) –
June 30, 1862
Malvern Hill – July 1, 1862

changing its supply line south to the James River and, at the same time, trying to beat off the attacks of the pursuing Confederates.

In the next three days, three more battles were fought. On June 29 the Battle of Savage's Station was fought. Essentially it was a rear-guard action in which the Confederates were repulsed. The following day another rear-guard action occurred near Glendale. Again the Confederates failed to break through and again the Union forces retired during the night.

The final battle was fought at Malvern Hill. The Union position was very strong and should not have been assaulted. In fact, General Lee almost decided not to make the attempt. Late in the afternoon, however, when he thought the Union troops were retiring, he ordered an attack which was decisively repulsed. The next day the Union troops retreated to Harrison's Landing in the historic James River plantation area. Shortly thereafter Lee returned to Richmond.

In the Seven Days Battle the Confederate army numbered about 85,000 against over 100,000 Union troops, and yet General Lee had managed to maintain the offensive throughout, pushing the Union army to the southeast in a great curve, stretching from Mechanicsville to Malvern Hill. The threat to Richmond vanished. The prestige and morale of the Army of Northern Virginia was completely restored.

On the other hand, the Union Army of the Potomac had fought well. Its commander had placed it in a poor position astride the Chickahominy, inviting attack. Its retreat had been conducted in an outstanding manner. In a sense, General McClellan somewhat redeemed himself by his excellent work of the last three days. In another sense this simply illustrates wherein his talents lay; a good organizer, he could also conduct an excellent retreat.

In addition, McClellan's corps commanders had all served him well, especially General Porter. Their opposite numbers had not done as well for Lee. Many of the Confederate attacks had been delivered without proper coordination, and as a result most of them had failed. This is, of course, reflected in the casualties sustained. The Union forces suffered almost 16,000 killed, wounded, captured or missing whereas the Confederates lost approximately 20,000 but acquired fifty-two guns and over thirty thousand small arms. One thing more should be added. The soldiers in the ranks were no longer recruits. A year's training and the combat of the last few days had made a radical change.

The Second Manassas Campaign

BY concentrating all of his available troops for the Seven Days Battle, General Lee had saved the Confederate capital from capture. He had driven McClellan and the Union Army of the Potomac away from Richmond but, in so doing, had left the rest of Virginia unguarded. He had been forced to ignore all the other Union troops scattered in various places in the northern part of the State.

In the meantime, President Lincoln had realized that these should be consolidated and put to some useful purpose. He called Major General John Pope, of Island No. 10 fame, from the West and gave him the command. Pope was junior in rank to three of the generals concerned, but only one of them objected. General Fremont resigned in a huff. This did not upset General Pope. He immediately set to work to organize his new command and at the same time he managed to irritate them by making a number of uncomplimentary comparisons between the troops in the East and the West. In an effort to indicate that he would wage an aggressive campaign he announced that his headquarters would be in the saddle. This proclamation tickled the fancy of the Confederates who remarked that that was where most people kept their hindquarters.

A few days after Pope took command of his new army, President Lincoln appointed a commander of all the Union armies. It had become obvious to him that he must have a military man in Washington. The events of the last few months in Virginia, with the Secretary of War trying to direct operations, had not been successful. The choice fell upon General "Old Brains" Halleck who had just captured Corinth, Miss. It was a logical choice for the President but not a particularly fortunate one, as we shall see. The fact that Lincoln recognized the necessity for a general in chief in Washington was a step in the right direction.

The first thing that Halleck did was to visit McClellan and order his army brought back nearer Washington. His object was to unite it eventually with General Pope's army. McClellan protested strenuously but finally started homeward. At that time General Pope was near Culpeper, still trying to group his forces together. Apparently it did not occur to General Halleck to consider the fact that General Lee's forces were directly between the two Union armies. Or, if he did think of this factor, he may have assumed that General Lee would stay where he was, guarding Richmond. We have already observed that Halleck was inclined to fight in terms of cities rather than to destroy the enemy armies. Furthermore, Halleck was, by nature, a very cautious individual. For political reasons he could not afford to leave his capital city unprotected, and certainly there was a lot to be said for this line of reasoning. But General Halleck's new opponent was destined to be marked in history as one of the greatest and most daring generals the world has ever known.

We have all seen pictures of General Robert E. Lee mounted on his splendid, gray horse, "Traveler." The very memory of these paintings or photographs is sufficient to call to mind his well-known qualities of infinite tact and patience, his calmness and serenity of purpose. This man, by his very bearing, was a true leader. We remember also the trust and devotion that he inspired in his army, inducing officers and men alike to undertake more than seemed humanly possible. We are inclined to forget that this man could be daring almost to an extreme. When the situation arose he could, and did, take remarkable chances with energy, resolution, and confidence. History also tells us that he showed kindness, sympathy, and understanding of human nature in the treatment of his own men—and an unusual talent for understanding his opponents. He would take far greater risks against McClellan, Halleck, or Pope than he would against Grant.

Early in August, General Lee sent Stonewall Jackson to

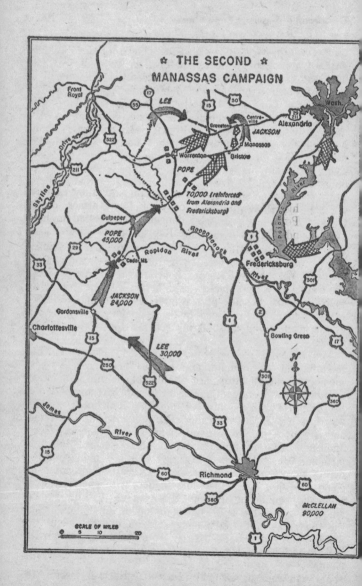

☆ THE SECOND ☆
MANASSAS CAMPAIGN

Front Royal

Wash.

LEE

Centreville
Groveton
JACKSON
Alexandria

Warrenton
Manassas
Bristow
POPE

70,000 (reinforced from Alexandria and Fredericksburg)

Culpeper

Rappahannock

POPE
45,000

Rapidan River

Cedar Mt.

Fredericksburg

River

JACKSON
24,000

Bowling Green

Gordonsville

Charlottesville

LEE
30,000

James

River

Richmond

McCLELLAN
90,000

SCALE OF MILES
0   5   10   20

Gordonsville. At Cedar Mountain (six miles south of Culpeper near the present U.S. Highway 15) Jackson attacked and defeated a part of Pope's army. This foretaste of events to come did not perturb either Pope or Halleck. They still assumed that Lee would remain near Richmond and, after all, General Pope had 45,000 men against Jackson's 24,000.

With 30,000 men General Lee left Richmond and headed for Gordonsville. Together with Jackson, his army now outnumbered Pope five to four. That the Union force escaped destruction is apparently only due to chance. A small Union cavalry column almost captured Jeb Stuart, now a Major General; they did get the first edition of his famous hat with the ostrich plume. More important still, they captured one of his officers with a copy of Lee's attack orders. General Pope finally saw his danger and retreated in haste to a second position behind the Rappahannock River.

In the meantime McClellan's army was being brought around by water; some landed at Alexandria and others came ashore near Fredericksburg. As soon as the Union troops debarked they were rushed to reinforce Pope. Why that general waited in place for them to join him is completely mystifying. He should have retreated toward Washington to meet them. Once the armies of McClellan and Pope were combined they would heavily outnumber the Confederates. General Lee knew this only too well and was vainly trying to bring Pope to battle before the Union army became too strong. At this juncture Jeb Stuart took revenge for the loss of his prized hat. He conducted a raid in the Union rear and made off with Pope's best uniform coat. Of more value to Lee was the capture of a copy of Pope's orders and the correspondence, giving the location of his troops and the reinforcements hurrying to meet him. In two days Pope would have 70,000 men and shortly thereafter he would have over 100,000.

In the face of such an emergency, General Lee did an amazing thing. He divided his army in two, sending Jackson on a long march completely around the Union right flank, then down in the Union rear. Jackson started on August 25. He reached Bristow (formerly Bristoe Station) at about sunset on August 26, a most remarkable feat even for the famous "foot-cavalry." They covered nearly sixty miles in two days, over badly rutted country roads in the hot August sun.

For months these men had been constantly marching and fighting; their clothing and shoes were gone; many made this long, gruelling march barefooted. From Bristow they went to Manassas, where they found undreamed of wealth, huge storage depots of the Union army—shoes, food, more supplies than they could possibly use. Many Union generals, during the course of the war, remarked upon the overabundance of supplies accumulated for the Army of the Potomac. This time they went to some soldiers who really needed them.

That same day Lee started to follow Jackson but Pope did nothing. The following day, August 27, Pope started to retreat. At some time on this day he may have realized what a marvelous opportunity Lee had given him of placing the Union army between the two wings of the Confederates and destroying them in turn. At any rate he started his forces in the right direction to cut off Jackson's retreat. Then he heard that Jackson was at Manassas, so he started for Manassas, assuming Jackson would wait for him. Later, news came in that Jackson was at Centreville, so he started for that place. And so it went, Union troops marching and countermarching, becoming more and more tired while Pope hunted in vain for Jackson and his men.

Finally, on the evening of August 28, Jackson revealed his position by attacking some troops passing in front of him on the present U.S. Highway 29 at a place called Groveton. This action precipitated the Second Battle of Manassas, to be fought out in the next two days.

The Second Battle of Manassas

THE Confederate situation at the opening of this battle is simple to describe. General Lee had divided his army into two parts, sending Stonewall Jackson ahead on a raid to the rear of the Union army. On the morning of August 29, Jackson was in position on the north side of the Warrenton Turnpike (U.S. 29 & 211). Lee, with Longstreet's troops, was hurrying to join his forces together for the coming battle.

The Union army was, however, badly scattered and the men were tired. For two days General Pope had been vainly searching for Jackson, marching back and forth, heading for wherever he had been last reported. The preceding evening Jackson had attacked a Union division at Groveton (where the Dogan House still stands beside the highway). So Pope turned his army around again and started for that place, thinking Jackson was still retreating.

This time, however, Jackson was waiting for him. In fact he had deliberately revealed his position. He must bring on a battle before Pope was reinforced, even though Lee had not yet arrived on the scene. That was the purpose of Lee's sending him forward by himself—to confuse Pope and force him into battle. Stonewall Jackson had accomplished both assignments; Pope had a completely false idea of the situation and the fight was soon to begin, but Lee and Longstreet must arrive on time.

The first day's battle (August 29, 1862) consisted of a series of furious Union assaults against Jackson's position, all of which were repulsed. No general attack was made, no effort was made to turn Jackson's north (left) flank. Pope

THE SECOND
☆ BATTLE OF ☆
MANASSAS

Sudley
Church

Bull Run

Stone
Bridge

Stone
House

Turnpike

Warrenton

Confederate
Cemetery

Dogan
House

Groveton

Iron Gates

Bald

Hill

Chinn
House

Henry
House

Manassas Sudley Road

New Market

Mt. Pone

To Manassas

SCALE OF MILES

0   .5   1

LEGEND:

National Military Park
Headquarters

Union attacks Aug. 29, 1862

Union attack Aug. 30, 1862

Confederate attacks Aug. 30

ROADS   TRAILS

Civil War Routes - - -

Modern Routes - - -

Old & New Routes
Coinciding

simply threw in his troops piecemeal as they arrived on the scene. He did order one of his corps commanders to attack Jackson's south (right) flank but this order became impossible to execute. Before the Union corps could get into position General Lee arrived and placed Longstreet's men on that side of Jackson's line.

The Union corps commander was the same Fitz-John Porter, now a major general, who had fought so well for the Union cause at the Seven Days Battle. For his failure to obey this impossible order he was later court-martialed and dismissed from the service. Unquestionably, Pope made a scapegoat of him. Porter was to spend the rest of his life trying to vindicate himself. Many years later he was given another hearing, acquitted, and restored to his rank.

The morning of the second day, August 30, passed rather uneventfully. Then, for some reason or other, General Pope decided that Lee was retreating so launched another attack just north of the Turnpike. From beginning to end, Pope's every guess seems to have been wrong. Well-placed, massed Confederate artillery broke the first Union assaults but the Northern troops reformed and kept moving bravely forward, regardless of losses. Some of Jackson's men ran out of ammunition and resorted to clubbed muskets and rocks. The fighting here was particularly bitter and prolonged. The Union forces were not finally repulsed until some of Longstreet's men were brought over from the other flank, to hurl themselves into the fray.

At this juncture Longstreet moved forward to capture Bald Hill, a commanding position with a fine view of a large part of the battlefield, which had been left almost unguarded. Union troops hastened from across the road, south to the Henry House Hill. If they lost that position their escape route over the Stone Bridge would be cut. Longstreet fought to capture it but the Northern ranks held firm. In this battle the original Henry House, which had been badly damaged in the first battle, was completely destroyed. Finding that the troops to his front had been weakened by the sending of units across to the Henry House Hill, Jackson then moved forward with a rush and ended the battle by driving the remainder of the Union army from the field. Three days later the Union forces retired into the defenses of Washington.

In this battle the Union army had a force of over 70,000

men present but only about 63,000 were actually engaged. The other were guarding the baggage trains and did not reach the scene. Their casualties, including a high percentage of prisoners, totaled about 14,000. General Lee's army of about 54,000 was fully employed, suffered something less than 10,000 casualties, and captured thirty guns and thousands of small arms.

The Campaign of Antietam

AFTER driving the Union army back into the defenses of Washington, General Lee wasted no time. He knew full well that he could not possibly capture the city either by siege or by assault. It was too strongly fortified and furthermore most of McClellan's troops from the Peninsula were now in Washington. Together with what was left of Pope's army, they far outnumbered his own force.

General Lee then embarked on his first invasion of the North. His main purpose in doing so was political. The peace party in the North was claiming that the war was a failure and at the moment it certainly appeared to be. The State of Maryland was supposed to contain many Southern sympathizers who would flock to the colors. Furthermore, an invasion should help in obtaining foreign recognition of the Confederacy.

The Army of Northern Virginia numbering about 55,000 men crossed the Potomac near Leesburg. Most of the men went via White's Ford close to where the ferry boat *Jubal A. Early* now runs, carrying cars back and forth over the river. With Stonewall Jackson in the lead, the Confederates then struck out for Frederick, Maryland. To their disappointment very few recruits came to join them, for the people of the State of Maryland were not as strongly in favor of secession as the Confederates had supposed. Perhaps the rugged, ragged appearance of the Southern soldiers when contrasted with the well-fed, well-clothed Northern soldiers acted as a deterrent to enlistment. Incidentally, it was at Frederick that the famous Barbara Fritchie incident

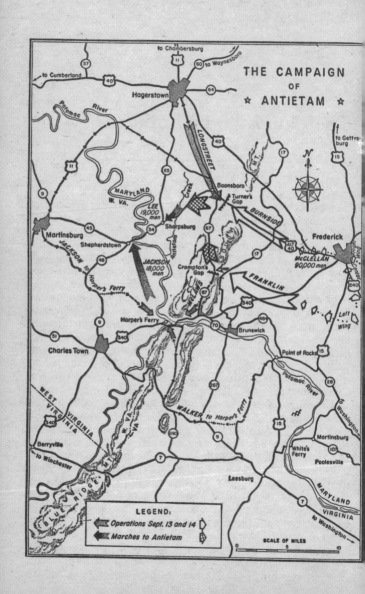

THE CAMPAIGN
OF
☆ ANTIETAM ☆

LEGEND:
⬅ Operations Sept. 13 and 14
⬅ Marches to Antietam

SCALE OF MILES
0   5   10

is supposed to have occurred. Of course the story is just a myth but Whittier made it into a stirring poem.

Meanwhile, in the Union capital all was doubt and confusion. McClellan was in command of the Union Army of the Potomac, Halleck still acting as commander of all the Union armies. With two such cautious men in charge practically nothing was done except to be sure that the Union army stayed between Lee and the capital. There was, however, one difference of opinion between them. At Harper's Ferry there was a strong Union garrison which McClellan wanted to withdraw. Surrounded by mountains, the place was absolutely indefensible; the garrison should have been withdrawn, but Halleck would not permit it. General Lee decided that his supply line should be via the Shenandoah Valley, and so it was essential to capture Harper's Ferry. This decision and the method of accomplishing it was to affect the whole campaign.

On September 9, 1862, General Lee issued his now-famous Special Orders No. 191. Three different columns were to converge on Harper's Ferry from three different directions while the remainder of the army marched westward across South Mountain. Splitting his army into four different parts was risky in the face of a Union force of 90,000 men, but Lee felt sure of his opponent. If he could divide the army into two parts in front of Pope, he could surely take even greater risks in front of McClellan.

Everything went according to plan. The four Confederate columns went their separate directions without any undue interference from anyone. Meanwhile, McClellan's army was marching very slowly and cautiously, feeling its way from Washington toward Frederick. Shortly after noon on Semptember 13, a copy of Special Orders No. 191 came into McClellan's hands. It was addressed to Major General D. H. Hill and had been found wrapped around three cigars at an abandoned campsite. The question as to who was responsible for such strange treatment of such an important document has long been the subject of controversy, but it matters little now. Here was a golden opportunity for McClellan to destroy the Southern army, before it could come together again, by striking the two groups north of the Potomac immediately.

South Mountain was the key to the situation. By marching

immediately the Union army should be able to get through the gaps before Lee's army was aware of its danger. McClellan should have marched that very night but he waited until morning. And that same night Lee learned from Jeb Stuart that McClellan had found a copy of his order. General Lee promptly started every available man for Turner's Gap. When the Union troops under Major General Burnside arrived it took all day and part of the night to fight their way through. At Crampton's Gap, farther to the south, Major General Franklin's men also had to fight their way through, which they accomplished by nightfall.

General Lee had gained a day by the fighting in the mountain passes, but he was still in a perilous position. He did not know whether or not Harper's Ferry had yet been captured. He had with him only 19,000 men. There was only one possible course of action open: he must retreat, and fast. He headed for the Potomac near Sharpsburg. As he reached that town a message came from Stonewall Jackson that Harper's Ferry, with its garrison of 11,000 men, had been captured. Jackson was en route to join him. Quickly the army turned, formed line of battle behind Antietam Creek and faced their enemy. This was September 15 but McClellan, following leisurely, did not attack until September 17, thereby giving time for the Confederates from Harper's Ferry to join, though it took hard marching, night and day, to do it. Three Confederate divisions arrived on the 16th; two more came on the morning of the 17th. The last division, commanded by Major General A. P. Hill, had been left to arrange for the surrender of Harper's Ferry. Even his men arrived in time to play a crucial part in the battle.

The Battle of Antietam

WHEN, on September 15, 1862, General Lee stopped to
fight at Antietam he must have known that he was taking
a considerable risk. Stonewall Jackson's message told him that
the rest of the Confederate army was hastening to join. When
they all arrived Lee would have under his command nearly
40,000 men. In the meantime, however, he had only about
19,000 and there were from 70,000 to 90,000 Union troops
nearby.

Despite these dangerous odds General Lee unhesitatingly
stopped the retreat and formed his line of battle. The
position in which the Confederates found themselves was
not strong, defensively. Their right flank was behind Antietam Creek which could be easily forded. Their left flank
was in some woods north of the village of Sharpsburg on
the road to Hagerstown (State Highway 65). Between these
two points the line stretched across low hills, through a
number of farms and thinly wooded areas. There were not
enough men to hold this line and, furthermore, the hills to
the east were higher. Artillery posted there could dominate
the area. To their rear was the Potomac River. If they were
defeated and forced back there could be no escape.

Stonewall Jackson and the rest of the Confederates were
many miles away. Could they possibly arrive before the
Union army, most of which was much closer? General Lee
must have thought they could; surely he counted on the
fact that Jackson would move fast while McClellan would
be slow and hesitant to move at all. And yet, even if everyone were to arrive at the same time, the Confederates would

91

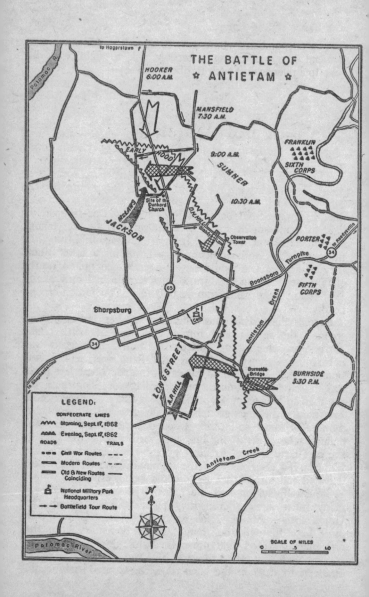

still be outnumbered about two to one. It would seem that General Lee was taking a terrible risk to fight with his back to a river against such terrific odds.

The Battle of Antietam should have been fought on the next day, September 16. The Union army could have reached the field in force. If it had done so, there would have been only Lee's 19,000 plus about one half of Jackson's to oppose it; three division were still en route. There was a small amount of skirmishing that day but only one Union corps, that under Major General Joseph Hooker, was involved.

The battle, which the North calls Antietam because of the creek, and which the South named Sharpsburg for the village, began at dawn on September 17, 1862. We can trace its progress more easily if we remember it as a series of five separate Union attacks from right to left. First came General Hooker's Corps of three division. It forced the Southern line back but, after desperate fighting lasting over an hour, was itself forced back. The brunt of this assault was borne by Major General John B. Hood's and Brigadier General Jubal A. Early's Confederate Divisions.

This was the end of the battle for Hooker's men but not for Hood's or Early's. Barely had they repulsed the first attack when they were struck again by General Mansfield's Union Corps. Although Mansfield himself was killed almost instantly his men drove valiantly forward to capture the Dunkard Church. Here the fighting raged for another hour and a half. The Union troops could advance no farther; the Confederate lines held but their situation was desperate. A few reinforcements had been sent from the right flank but losses had been terrific, not only from the infantry fighting, but also from heavy artillery fire from those high hills to the east.

The third attack of the day was made by only one Union division, part of another corps which had just arrived on the field. The corps commander, General Sumner, did not wait for his other division but plunged straight into the fight for the Dunkard Church. Meanwhile, two more Confederate division had arrived on the field after marching all night. They were allowed to rest for one hour then were sent into the lines. One of these, General McLaw's Division, marched to the very spot where General Sumner was pushing forward. Only the timely arrival of these men stopped this third attack. The Union troops now found themselves caught in a pocket. In a matter of minutes over 2000 men fell. This ended the attacks on the Confederate left flank.

The fourth Union attack by the other two divisions of Sumner's Corps was already in progress. It was met by Major General D. H. Hill's troops at a sunken road about the middle of the Confederate position. If possible, the fight was more bitter and desperate here than it had been on the left. It is no wonder that this was called The Bloody Lane. Eventually the attacking Union troops, pushing resolutely forward in the face of terrific rifle and cannon fire, reached a position near the site of the large Observation Tower, which gives such an excellent view of the battlefield today. From here, they could shoot down the whole length of the Confederate line at the sunken road. At this crucial moment the colonel of the nearest Confederate regiment, John B. Gordon, was lying unconscious, having been wounded five times already that day. The lieutenant colonel, intending to pull the right wing back to face the enveloping Union troops, gave the command, "About Face; Forward March." The effects of this one unfortunate command spread to the whole brigade, which broke and fled. All that was needed was one vigorous Union charge and it might have meant the end of Lee's whole army. Amazingly, it never came.

Although no one yet knew it, the battle was over except on the Confederate right. On this flank Major General Burnside had been given the task of assaulting the Confederate line. During the morning he had made several unsuccessful attempts to dash across the creek over the bridge which now bears his name, but had been repulsed every time. Why he did not simply have his men wade across the little creek has never been satisfactorily explained. Finally, about 1:00 p.m., his troops rushed the Burnside Bridge again and captured it, to find that almost all of the Confederates to their front had already been withdrawn to the hills above. In fact, there were very few Confederates left in that entire sector, for most of them had been sent to fight on other parts of the field. For two more hours Burnside waited, gathering his forces for the attack. Finally at about 3:00 p.m. he started moving slowly up the hill. In about an hour his men were actually in the streets of Sharpsburg. There was practically no one left to oppose him. Victory seemed certain; General Lee did not have a single unit in reserve to stop Burnside's advance.

But Burnside had been too slow. Someone else has been too fast. Starting that same morning seventeen miles away at Harper's Ferry, General A. P. Hill, wearing his red battle shirt, urging his men forward with drawn sword, marching furiously with colors flying, had come with his division to fall upon the Union flank and drive it back to Antietam Creek. The battle was over, all along the line.

Most historians agree that at the battle of Antietam more men were killed and wounded than on any other one day in the entire Civil War. The Confederate losses were about 10,000, one fourth of those engaged. The Union losses were over 12,000, also about one fourth. General McClellan had not employed all his troops: two Union corps stood idle and took no part in the battle. McClellan had available more than 70,000 men yet used only about 46,000.

Surely on the next day General McClellan could be expected to renew the battle. Although he had not won on the 17th his men had inflicted terrible losses on the Confederates. The Union army had fought much better than had its commander. He had let it deliver five separate and uncoordinated attacks. One large, well-planned assault on the 18th, delivered with fresh troops would certainly finish Lee's army.

In the Confederate camp all the other leaders urged an immediate retreat as the only way to save the army from disaster, and yet, on the morning of the 18th the army was still there inviting the attack which never came. General Lee knew his McClellan. He also knew his soldiers as no other man ever did. He was determined that the Army of Northern Virginia was not to believe that it had ever been driven from any field. It was not then, and it never was. Not until the night of September 18 did the Confederates retreat. By the next morning the last units were safely back across the Potomac. The first invasion of the North had failed.

From Antietam to Fredericksburg and Murfreesboro

IT IS remarkable how quickly the fortunes of war can change. In May, 1862, the end of the Confederacy had seemed very near. McClellan was knocking on the gates of Richmond, while in Mississippi, Halleck was slowly moving forward with a huge army. There seemed no way to stop either one. Suddenly all this had altered. By early September Lee was invading Maryland, Bragg was invading Kentucky, while Grant was hanging on as best he could to a small part of Mississippi.

Now Lee was retreating from Antietam, and on the very day that the last of his men crossed the Potomac, a battle was fought at Iuka, Mississippi. It was rather inconclusive but led to another battle two weeks later at Corinth which the South lost. Four days after that, on October 8, Bragg's invasion of Kentucky came to an end at the Battle of Perryville. Here the South claimed a victory, but it was not a decisive one. Both sides suffered very severely; but without an overwhelming success General Bragg could no more stay in Kentucky than Lee could in Maryland.

The pendulum had swung in favor of the North, then toward the South, then back to the middle. It would seem as if neither side had gained anything by all their strenuous efforts. The situation in Virginia, West Virginia, Kentucky, and east Tennessee was about as it had been several months earlier. This state of affairs was exactly what the South was fighting for; if the North could not conquer her in a reasonable length of time the mass of the people might agree that the war was not worth continuing and let the Confederacy go in peace. To keep the Northern Peace Party alert, Lee sent Stuart off on another raid around the Union army as far north as Chambersburg, Pennsylvania.

However, a glance at the map will show that the North had won something in Missouri and in Arkansas. Furthermore, the navy had captured a number of points along the coast, and along the line of the Mississippi the Union forces had made considerable progress. During the closing months of the year the Northern armies pushed forward again in the Mississippi Valley, in Virginia, and in middle Tennessee. Let us take these advances in the order in which they occurred and concentrate first on the Mississippi Valley region.

By now both the North and the South were fully aware of the importance of the Mississippi. If the North could gain control of the river the Confederacy would be split into two parts, each unable to help the other. There was only one great strongpoint left, but it was the largest and most powerful of them all—Vicksburg.

To this prize General Grant now turned. He planned to advance in two columns; one was to be commanded by Major General Sherman, the other was to be under his own direct control. From the very start his expedition ran into difficulty, not with the Confederates, but with the authorities in Washington. It was all very confusing; everybody seemed to be in favor of his capturing Vicksburg, but he could get no cooperation from higher authority, and the orders that he did receive were misleading or evasive. Eventually it developed that one of his subordinates, Major General McClernand, had been engaged in some political skulduggery. He wanted to organize the expedition that would capture Vicksburg and was busy pulling strings in Washington to get the Secretary of War to give him the command.

Of course, General Grant did not know of this intrigue but managed to get his troops started in spite of it. He marched overland, while Sherman went down the river by ship and landed just north of Vicksburg. On December 29, Sherman attacked the Confederate positions on Chickasaw Bluffs, but was severely repulsed. In the meantime Grant's overland expedition had also been stopped but for very different reasons. Two Confederate cavalry forces raided his line of communications so effectively that his men were put

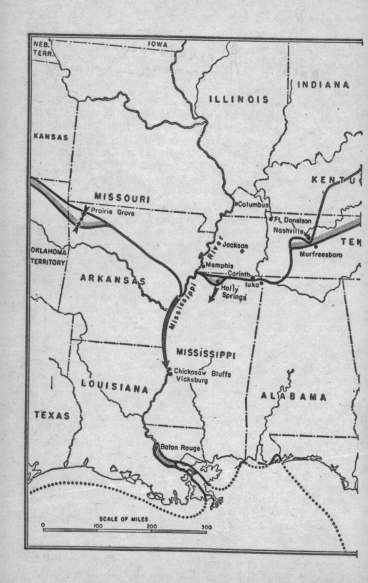

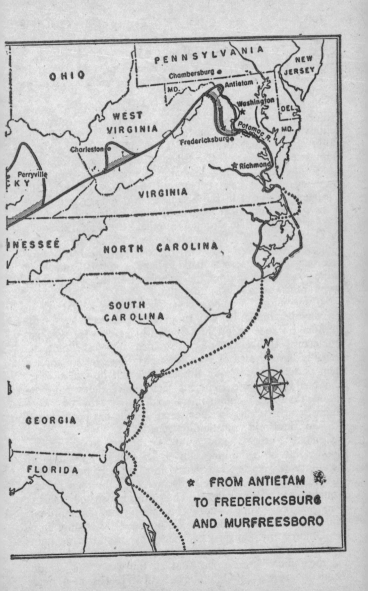

★ FROM ANTIETAM ★
TO FREDERICKSBURG
AND MURFREESBORO

on half rations and he was forced to turn back. The new Union depot at Holly Springs, Mississippi, was destroyed by a force under Major General Earl Van Dorn, while simultaneously Brigadier General Forrest caused more trouble farther north in Tennessee.

The latter was a remarkable cavalry exploit, but then Nathan Bedford Forrest was a remarkable man. He had received no military schooling, in fact he had very little formal education of any kind. When war came and his native state of Tennessee joined the Confederacy, Forrest promptly enlisted as a private. Soon thereafter he raised his own unit, supplying it to a great extent out of his own pocket (he had been successful in the business world too). At the time of his escape from Fort Donelson, when he led his men out in a sortie rather than surrender, he held the rank of colonel. By December, 1862, his reputation was well established on both sides. A rugged, powerful six foot two, he had already been engaged in several hand-to-hand combats, and been severely wounded. Before the war was over he was to have twenty-nine horses killed under him.

No one taught him how cavalry should be fought. From the very beginning he was thoroughly practical; he fought his men on foot or on horseback whichever was most advantageous. Unlike the officers trained at West Point, he probably never heard of Napoleon's Maxims, yet he applied them perfectly. Add to all this the fact that he was a leader who could get more from his men under the worst conditions than most commanders could under the best conditions, and it is easy to understand why he has been classed as one of the world's outstanding generals.

General Forrest's raid into Tennessee to break up Grant's line of communications is an excellent example of his ability as a leader. He started in mid-December of 1862 with troops he had only recently met (not the men he had brought into the service). These newly-assigned soldiers were poorly equipped, having practically no ammunition. Rifles, guns, and ammunition he obtained by capture from the Union army. Pursued constantly by overpowering numbers he continued capturing garrison after garrison, wrecking the railroad lines as he went all the way from Jackson, Tennessee nearly to Columbus, Kentucky. His men made terrifically long marches through bitterly cold, wet weather yet escaped with little loss. This raid, together with Van Dorn's at Holly Springs, effectively stopped General Grant's advance toward Vicksburg for the year 1862.

The Battle of Fredericksburg

AFTER the Battle of Antietam, the victorious Union Army of the Potomac made one unsuccessful attempt at pursuit, then left the Confederates unmolested. Lee's army spent the time resting and reorganizing, drilling new recruits, rebuilding its strength. James Longstreet and Stonewall Jackson were promoted to lieutenant generals. The Army of Northern Virginia was formed into two corps; Longstreet took command of the First, Jackson of the Second.

Except for Jeb Stuart's raid into Pennsylvania practically nothing occurred to disturb the soldiers of either army. The month of October, 1862 was probably one of the most pleasant of the whole war for the contending armies in the East. This was fine for the spirits of the men in the ranks, but the people of the North were becoming impatient. The Union army had repelled the Confederate invasion. Five days after the battle, on the 22nd of September, President Lincoln had seized the opportunity presented by the Union victory to issue his preliminary announcement of the Emancipation Proclamation, to become effective on the first of January, 1863. The Northern people, still not realizing how long and grim the struggle would be to subdue the South, sensed victory in the air and demanded action.

From a military point of view the Northern people were right. General McClellan should not have been content with simply repelling the invasion. The Union could never win this war by standing on the defensive. Yet it was the end of October before McClellan began to move. When he did cross the Potomac nothing happened. The President decided that he must find another commander. His choice was Major General Ambrose E. Burnside.

For many years it has been popular to criticize Lincoln for his selection of commanding generals of the Army of the Potomac, and General Burnside is the one most frequently chosen as an example. It is true that Burnside tried to refuse the appointment, and did not feel that he was capable. How could the President know whether or not this effort at refusal was a real confession of weakness or simple modesty? Lincoln's first choice had been McClellan fresh from victories in West Virginia, his second choice had been Pope, also fresh from victory on the Mississippi. Now, General Burnside was one of the senior corps commanders and he was the only one who had successfully conducted an independent operation, the seizure of a large part of the coast of North Carolina earlier in the year. This had been a simple task. There had been practically no one to oppose the Union troops who had landed with overwhelming numbers, yet it had been successful. Burnside might be the general the North so badly needed.

Immediately upon assuming command Burnside submitted his plan. It involved a simple, straightforward move on Fredericksburg, then an advance due south to Richmond. The success of the whole scheme depended upon moving the Union forces across the Rappahannock River and seizing the heights behind the city before Lee's army arrived. For this purpose pontoon bridging equipment was ordered to Fredericksburg. When the first Union troops arrived on the scene there was practically no one to oppose their crossing, but on account of a failure in the reception of orders the pontoons had not arrived. The river was fordable at the time but the water could rise. General Burnside would not permit the leading elements to cross lest they become isolated from the rest of the army. He decided to wait for the pontoons. By the time they reached the scene it was too late. Lee's army was also there.

For the battle soon to be fought, General Burnside had organized the Army of the Potomac into three Grand Divisions commanded by Generals Sumner, Hooker, and Franklin. The total Union force numbered about 120,000 men. Burnside's plan of attack was simple enough. Sumner's Right Grand Division was to cross on three pontoon bridges

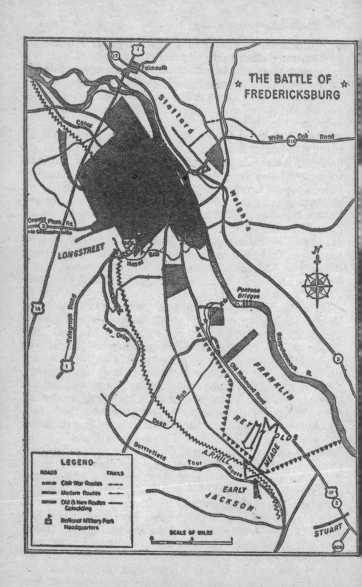

at Fredericksburg. Franklin's Left Grand Division was to cross on three other bridges farther downstream. Hooker was to support their attacks with some of his troops, while the rest were to remain on the north bank as a general reserve. The Union artillery was posted at Falmouth and on Stafford Heights, commanding positions which dominated the field of battle.

The Confederate army of about 78,000 waited on the south side of the river, but not along the water's edge. An open plain extends along the south bank, and an army there would have been exposed to the fire of the Union batteries. General Lee posted one brigade in the city itself, but the bulk of the Southern army was drawn up on the irregular edge of a plateau running generally parallel to the river. The left of the line was held by Longstreet's Corps, the right by Jackson's. The left was by far the stronger part of the line, for it rested on a steep elevation known as Marye's Heights. In front of the position was a wide canal and a drainage ditch which the Union troops would have to cross. Behind the ditch, at the base of the hill, there was also an old sunken road with, in front of it, an old stone wall just the right height to protect the defending troops while they shot over it.

Marye's Heights are now well within the present city limits of Fredericksburg. The National Cemetery is located on the top of the hill, the Park Headquarters at the foot. The old sunken road was right between the two. A portion of the old stone wall, reconstructed in 1939, marks the exact location. All of these are just north of the present U.S. Highway 1, which used to be known here as the Telegraph Road.

On December 11 the Union army started to build its pontoon bridges across the river. On the Union left, where there was no opposition, the three pontoon bridges were quickly laid, in spite of the fact that the ice in the river was half an inch thick. At Fredericksburg, however, the first attempt was a complete failure. No troops had been sent across the river to protect the bridgebuilders while they worked. The Confederate brigade in the city simply shot the engineers off their pontoons. The Union artillery then shelled the city for over an hour to try to drive out the Confederates, but it was not until troops were ferried across the river that the bridges could be laid. By evening of the next day all except that portion of Hooker's Grand Division in general reserve had crossed the river and were ready to assault the Confederate position. During the night it was agreed that the Union main attack would be launched against Jackson's Corps on the Confederate right. This was certainly the proper choice. Here there was no ditch, no sunken road, stone wall, or drainage canal. There was only a long, low ridge, heavily wooded. The present-day Battlefield Tour Route (Lee Drive) follows closely behind the Confederate lines on this flank. The terrain in this section has been carefully preserved.

Early in the morning of December 13 General Burnside changed his mind. Instead of attacking with his whole Left Grand Division only a part was to move forward. Under cover of a dense fog, one division, Major General George G. Meade's, advanced from the line of the Old Richmond Road (now U.S. Highway 17), supported on right and left by two others. Not until the fog lifted, could the Confederates actually see that they were about to be attacked. Then occurred the extraordinary exploit of the youthful Major Pelham of Jeb Stuart's horse artillery. With only two guns, one of which was soon disabled, he galloped to the Confederate right flank in front of the lines and with one gun section delayed the Union advance for half an hour. He and his men fought four Union batteries until their ammunition was almost gone, then galloped back to safety.

The Union troops again advanced but were again stopped when Jackson's artillery opened fire. Then the Union guns on Stafford Heights joined in. There ensued an artillery duel lasting an hour and a half. Jackson's artillery was eventually silenced. Meade's troops rushed forward and by good fortune found a weak spot in the Confederate line. If the whole Union Left Grand Division had been present as originally planned, the battle of Fredericksburg might have had a different ending. Alone, Meade's troops could not hold the ground they had taken. The Confederates under Generals Early and A. P. Hill counterattacked and regained their position, but were themselves checked when they tried to advance.

At the opposite end of the battlefield the Union troops, first Sumner's men, then Hooker's, assaulted Marye's Heights with incredible bravery, not just once but fourteen times. They came within twenty-five yards of the stone wall but could go no farther. Everyone knew that the effort was hopeless, but Burnside issued orders to renew the attack the next day. Eventually his commanders persuaded him to give up the effort. Two nights later the Union army retreated across the river to the north bank.

Many historians believe that General Lee lost at Fredericksburg his best chance to destroy the Union army, that he should have counterattacked on the evening of the battle while the Northern forces were disorganized from their defeat. Perhaps fate had a hand in the preservation of the Union. Lee had captured a copy of Burnside's attack order for the next day and therefore decided to wait until after that assault had been repulsed. By the next morning it was too late, the Union troops were by that time prepared to resist a counterattack.

The Confederate losses in this battle totaled 5300 killed and wounded, while the Union losses were over twice as great, about 12,600 men.

The Battle of Murfreesboro

AFTER his unsuccessful invasion of Kentucky in September and October, General Braxton Bragg moved to Murfreesboro, Tennessee, to await further developments. The Union Army of the Cumberland concentrated at Nashville, thirty-two miles to the northwest.

Although the Confederate invasion of Kentucky had not accomplished much, except to scare the people of the North for a while, the Union commander had lost the confidence of the administration in Washington. General Buell was replaced by Major General William S. Rosecrans. At the time of his appointment it was made clear to Rosecrans that he was expected to take prompt action to destroy the Confederate forces in Tennessee, but instead of advancing promptly against his enemy, General Rosecrans slowly and carefully began to gather supplies. He knew full well that the railroads in his rear were open to attack at any time by Confederate cavalry, and he did not propose to advance southward until he was completely equipped and completely ready.

For over a month the army stayed at Nashville while Rosecrans filled his wagon trains with two million rations and the administration screamed for action. From Washington, General Halleck wrote that unless he advanced immediately he would surely be relieved from command before he ever fought a battle. To this, Rosecrans replied that if they did not trust him they should replace him. If they left him in command he would do his duty as he saw best. Of course, Rosecrans was not relieved. How could Halleck, who was not on the ground to see the actual conditions, dictate the correct time of movement to the general in the field? Although we shall not find the name of Rosecrans listed among the great of the Civil War, we should remember him as a conscientious soldier who saw his proper duty and did his best to perform it, at whatever risk to his career. General Halleck backed down, rather ungraciously.

When he was ready, on December 26, 1862, General Rosecrans advanced toward Murfreesboro. It was a simple straightforward move in three parallel columns which Rosecrans designated as the Right, Center, and Left Wings. However, it took the Union army three days to reach the Confederate positions. Brigadier General Joe Wheeler's cavalry delayed them constantly, forcing the Union soldiers to deploy off the roads, fight their way across country, re-form on the roads, then deploy again. Throughout these three days, General Bragg was kept completely and accurately informed. It was not until late afternoon of December 29 that any part of the Union army reached the vicinity of Stones River where the battle was to be fought. The entire army did not get into position until the following day.

Marching with those Union columns we find a young brigadier general who, on this field of battle, was to make a name for himself. Here we find him as a division commander of infantry in the Right Wing, yet it is as a cavalry leader that he is to become famous. Philip H. Sheridan fought so vigorously and so impulsively that in later years Grant picked him for these same qualities to lead the U.S. cavalry in the East, regardless of his extensive infantry experience. Swarthy, black-haired, short of stature, overfull of energy, Sheridan was always in the forefront of every battle. His men, watching him, followed and trusted him in defeat as in victory. Here, at Murfreesboro, it was to be defeat, but he would fight well.

Awaiting the advance of the Union forces, the Confederate Army of Tennessee stood along the general line of Stones River, about two miles northwest of the city. This is another instance of a battle with two names. To the North it became known as the Battle of Stones River. The South was to call it the Battle of Murfreesboro (old spelling Murfreesborough).

The river itself is comparatively small and easily fordable at many places. It did not constitute a serious obstacle to the movement of troops, and during the battle units of both armies crossed and recrossed it more than once. General Bragg, therefore, did not hesitate to dispose his army on both sides of the river. His object was not to used the river as an obstacle but to place his army in front of Murfreesboro, covering the roads which the Union forces must take in order to reach the city. Part of the Confederate force was on the right bank, the bulk of it was in front of the river on the left bank.

The Battle of Murfreesboro is similar to the first Battle of Manassas in one peculiar way. Each army, unbeknownst to the other, planned to attack the opposite flank of the enemy. In this case, each planned to attack the other's right. Which would succeed might well depend on which started first. In the early morning of December 31, 1862, the Confederates made the first move. Their plan was to advance with Lieutenant General Hardee's Corps on the left, swing northward, and roll up the Union line. Lieutenant General "Bishop" Polk's Corps in the center was then to join in the assault. One division, the one on the opposite side of the river, under Major General Breckinridge, was to act as a sort of general reserve.

At the beginning the Confederate attack went exceedingly well. Charging through the thick cedar thickets, which covered the battlefield, they soon sent the first two divisions of the Union Right Wing (Major General McCook in command) reeling backward. Outstanding in these assaults was an extremely brave, resourceful Confederate major general named Cleburne. A leader of the sort that men will follow in any charge, he had already proved his worth at Shiloh in combat against Sherman and his troops. From now on Pat Cleburne will be found in the thick of every battle of the Confederate Army of Tennessee.

Having rolled up the first two divisions, the Confederates pressed eagerly forward hoping to do the same to the rest, only to find the next division more stubborn. General Sheridan refused to give ground so easily, in fact, he even counterattacked. He then re-formed on a new line at right angles to the old one and held his ground. We are reminded here of General Sherman at Shiloh; these two seem to have been cast in the same mold.

By now the whole Union Center commanded by Major

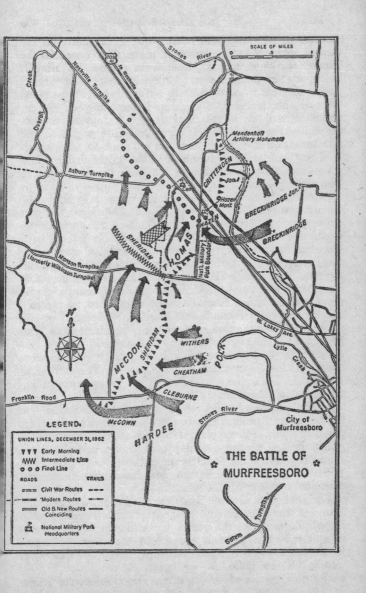

THE BATTLE OF
MURFREESBORO

LEGEND

UNION LINES, DECEMBER 31, 1862

▼▼▼ Early Morning

ⱮⱮⱮ Intermediate Line

○ ○ ○ Final Line

ROADS   TRAILS

━━━ Civil War Routes

━ ━ ━ Modern Routes

━━━ Old & New Routes
      Coinciding

🏳 National Military Park
    Headquarters

General George H. Thomas was engaged, reinforcing Sheridan's line. The Union attack across the river against the Confederate right flank had been hastily canceled. The Left Wing, under Major General Crittenden, was hurriedly retracing its steps to get to the scene of battle before it was too late. At this juncture, Sheridan's division ran out of ammunition and was forced to retire. Quick to seize the opportunity, the Confederates burst through the gap in the line and again the Northern forces fell back to a new position, just in front of and parallel to the old Nashville Turnpike. Here, with their back to the road, the Union forces prepared to make a final stand.

Now was the time for General Bragg to use his reserve. His other troops were tired but he still had Breckinridge's Division across the river. Bring it forward and attack the angle in the Union line and the battle could be finished. So it could have been but for two factors. Breckinridge was slow in moving, and Polk, to whom the attack was entrusted, committed the brigades piecemeal as they arrived. The Confederates suffered heavy losses and the Union brigade that bore the brunt of the assaults stood firm. The spot where General Hazen's Brigade held its ground and saved the Union army is marked today by the Hazen Monument, the oldest Civil War Monument on any field of battle.

Although no one then knew it, the battle of Murfreesboro had, for all practical purposes, ended. The next day, January 1, 1863, the two forces stood facing each other, neither taking any decisive action.

In the afternoon, Union troops crossed the river. On the following day Breckinridge, who had also recrossed, attacked them and drove them back. His own attack was then repulsed by the massed fire of several Union batteries from across the river. The artillery monument marks this concentration of fifty-eight Union guns assembled under the command of Major Mendenhall.

The next night General Bragg retreated southward and the Army of the Cumberland walked into Murfreesboro. Although defeated in the actual battle, losing twenty-eight guns, the Northern forces had gained their immediate objective. Both the South and the North ended by claiming a victory. Of the 45,000 Union troops present about 13,000 were killed, wounded or captured. The Confederate losses were about 10,000 out of a total force of about 38,000 engaged.

Why, after December 31, didn't General Bragg follow up his victory? He seems to have simply waited while the situation gradually deteriorated until he was forced to order his disappointed army to retreat, handing the city of Murfreesboro to the North. This question can probably only be answered by a look at Braxton Bragg himself. He was a conscientious, hard-working officer, wholeheartedly devoted to the Confederate cause. He was also possessed of a natural aggressiveness. He believed in attacking first but, if he was not immediately successful he became dispirited and lost his temper, blaming his subordinates for things that went wrong. In fact, he was a hard taskmaster who was not at all liked by the men who served under him. On important occasions he saw only too clearly the things that had gone wrong while forgetting the successes of his own troops. He found it difficult, if not impossible, to look confidently forward to what could be eventual success. The net result might perhaps be summed up by saying that he was an intelligent, skillful planner but, in the execution of his plans, he was his own worst enemy.

From Fredericksburg and
Murfreesboro to Chancellorsville

THE disaster at Fredericksburg severely shook the morale of the Army of the Potomac. If they had ever felt any confidence in General Burnside, this defeat had shattered it forever. It was essential that the President choose another general. He selected Major General Hooker, nicknamed "Fighting Joe," the former commander of Burnside's Center Grand Division. As first priority, the new commander devoted his immediate attention to raising the morale of his army. He adopted a system of furloughs to stop desertions from the ranks which had reached alarming proportions. Gradually, he rebuilt the spirit of the Union army until it was again ready to take the field.

It was in early March of this year, 1863, that the celebrated Confederate raider, Captain (later Colonel) John S. Mosby, slipped several miles behind the Union lines at Fairfax, Virginia, less than twenty miles from Washington. Here he captured a brigadier general (whom he roused from his bed), two captains, thirty men, and fifty-eight horses. In this raid Mosby took with him only twenty-nine men, all of whom returned safely to the Confederate lines. It is said that President Lincoln regretted the loss of the horses more than the general; he could promote others to be brigadier generals.

During this same period Rosecrans, after the Battle of Murfreesboro, was also content to spend the next few months right where he was. For a while he had trouble even doing that. The Confederate cavalry constantly radied his supply lines, captured wagon trains, and kept his army on half rations for several weeks. During this same period, the Union

114

cavalry attempted a raid of its own into Georgia. They had the misfortune of having General Forrest assigned to intercept them. He pursued the Union cavalry day and night, finally capturing the whole brigade, about 1600 men. By using the old, old trick of marching his men around and around over the same ground, Forrest led the Union officers to believe that they were outnumbered three to one. He actually had with him less than 500 men.

Farther west, along the Mississippi, the Union forces were much more active. Fort Hindman, known to the Union army as Arkansas Post, was captured in January. Then, for the next three months General Grant and Admiral Porter tried vainly to find some method of reaching Vicksburg. By the end of April they did succeed in crossing the river but the story of their efforts properly belongs with the Vicksburg Campaign. Simultaneously the Union army and navy operating from New Orleans acquired another foothold father west in Louisiana—at Opelousas.

Along the Atlantic Coast the navy tightened its hold on the southern ports. The running of the blockade became a very dangerous business. In addition to their normal assigned duties the navy was also directed to attack the Confederate forts with their new ironclads. Naval commanders protested but no one in Washington listened. The new monitors had become, in the minds of many people, the answer to everything. The attacks on Fort McAllister, in Georgia, and Fort Sumter, at Charleston, South Carolina, failed, as was to be expected. The new ironclads could take a great deal of punishment but on the other hand they were not seaworthy and could not inflict serious damage on a large coastal fortification.

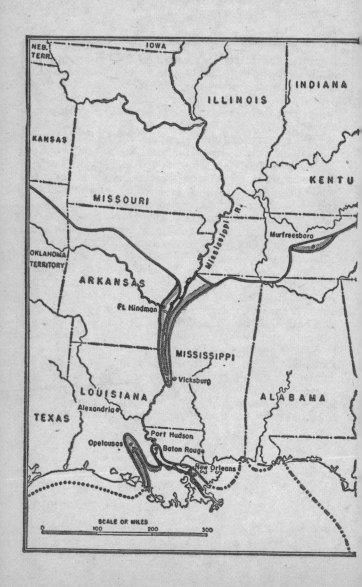

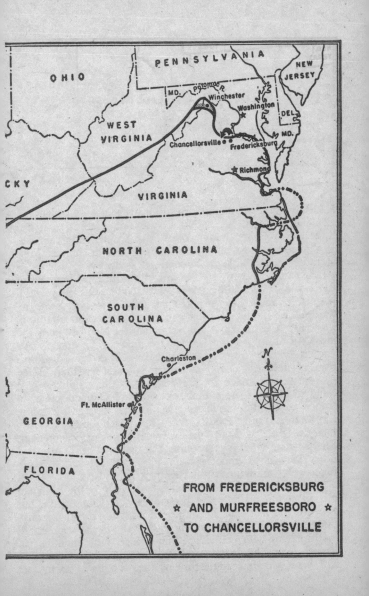

FROM FREDERICKSBURG
★ AND MURFREESBORO ★
TO CHANCELLORSVILLE

The Campaign and Battle
of Chancellorsville

FOR the student of military history the name Chancellorsville has a special fascination. It was not one battle; it was three battles—one Union victory, two Confederate victories. When an army defeats a well-trained, well-disciplined force of more than double its strength, it is an event worthy of careful study. When, at the same time, it furnishes one of the world's outstanding examples of courageous, resourceful leadership under adverse circumstances, it is even more rewarding. As if this were not enough to attract our attention, the name Chancellorsville also stands for the last, and the most daring, of all the Lee-Jackson maneuvers, dramatically grasping victory from apparent defeat. Never again was this team of great leaders and soldiers to function together. When Jackson fell wounded on the field of battle, a military epic came to an end. From that time forward General Lee continued to exhibit, again and again, the superb leadership, the strategic and tactical genius for which he is so justly famous. But, without the aid of his chief lieutenant, things were never again quite the same. The South had other very good generals who played their parts exceedingly well, but none could take Jackson's place.

On the Northern side, General "Fighting Joe" Hooker was in command. He had been a capable subordinate, but now for the first time he was faced with the awful responsibility of supreme command in battle. At first he approached his problems with confidence and ability. Four months had passed since the battle of Fredericksburg. Reinforcements had been received; the Army of the Potomac was in fact stronger than it had ever been, numbering 134,000 men. It was well trained, ready for battle, and considerably larger than any army the South had in the field. Its commander had every reason to feel confident.

As a matter of fact the Union army was more than twice as large as the Army of Northern Virginia. At the beginning of the Chancellorsville campaign, General Lee had with him around Fredericksburg fewer men than had taken part in the great battle there. Two divisions under the command of General Longstreet were absent, aiding in the defense of the Atlantic coast. The Confederate army on the scene numbered no more than 60,000 men.

Under such conditions it was only logical that General Hooker made the opening moves in the campaign. For these operations the Army of the Potomac was organized into seven corps. General Hooker's plan was to divide his army into two attack groups, one to threaten each flank of Lee's army. The main force consisting of three corps was to go on a long march, far to the west, then turn and approach Fredericksburg from that direction. The other attack group of two corps, under the command of Major General John Sedgwick, was meanwhile to cross below the city and attract Lee's attention to the eastward. The remaining two corps were held in reserve, guarding fords, ready to move to either flank as the situation developed.

The great flanking movement to the west started on April 27. Two days later all three of the Union corps involved had successfully crossed both the Rappahannock and the Rapidan. They were well beyond the Confederate left flank, marching east toward Fredericksburg, closing on Lee's army. As they came nearer they were to open up new fords and more direct routes for the Union reserves to cross the river. In anticipation of this event, the reserve corps were ordered to march toward the closer fords. Simultaneously, General Sedgwick began to cross below Fredericksburg with his two corps.

News of the flanking movement reached General Lee late on this same day, April 29. Yet the information was only fragmentary, he could not tell what it signified, but he could see General Sedgwick's troops crossing the river below the city. Nevertheless Lee dispatched Major General Richard H. Anderson with parts of his division to take command on the

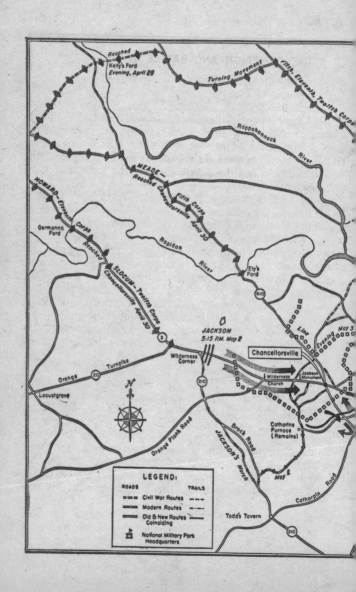

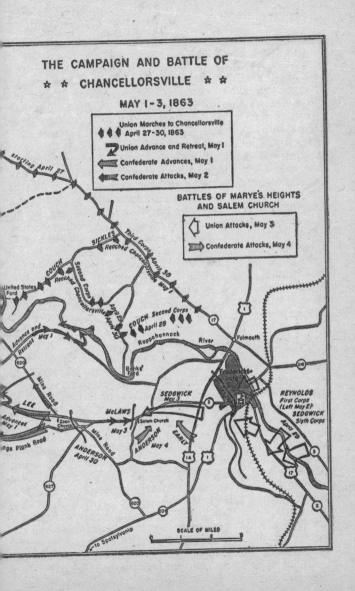

THE CAMPAIGN AND BATTLE OF
★ ★ CHANCELLORSVILLE ★ ★
MAY 1-3, 1863

Union Marches to Chancellorsville
April 27-30, 1863

Union Advance and Retreat, May 1

Confederate Advances, May 1

Confederate Attacks, May 2

BATTLES OF MARYE'S HEIGHTS
AND SALEM CHURCH

Union Attacks, May 3

Confederate Attacks, May 4

starting April 27

SICKLES

Third Corps April 30

Reached Chancellorsville May 1

COUCH

Reached Chancellorsville

Second Corps

April 29

April 30

COUCH Second Corps
April 28

United States
Ford

Rappahannock

River

Falmouth

17

1

Advance and
Retreat May 1

620

Banks
Ford

216

Fredericks-
burg

Mine Road

Zoan
Church

LEE

McLAWS

SEDGWICK
May 3

REYNOLDS
First Corps
(Left May 2)

5

SEDGWICK
Sixth Corps

Advances
May 1

May 3

Salem Church

April 29

ge Plank Road

Mine Road

ANDERSON May 4

EARLY

3

ANDERSON
April 30

1A

1

17

627

620

208

8

to Spotsylvania

SCALE OF MILES

0   1   2

left flank. During that night and early morning of April 30, Anderson collected his forces and began to entrench a line across the roads to the east of Chancellorsville, where the Mine Road meets the Orange Plank Road and the Orange Turnpike (State Highway 3). As news gradually filtered in to General Anderson, the situation must have seemed desperate to him, for on that same day the three Union corps that had made the wide flanking movement reached Chancellorsville and so did some of the union reserves (via the United States Ford). There he was with one lone Confederate division facing almost four Union corps. But his orders were to fight, and so there he stayed.

General Hooker arrived to take command of the forces at Chancellorsville, more confident than ever of success. His operations so far had proceeded exactly according to plan. Most of the Union army was now across the Rappahannock, threatening Lee's rear. It seemed that he would soon have the Confederates caught in a vise between his two attack groups. He halted for the night, losing valuable hours, never to be regained. By the time that he finally started to move again the next morning the situation had changed radically.

Let us turn back to General Lee again. By now he knew that a great force had been collected against his left flank and rear in the vicinity of Chancellorsville. The average general in his position, outflanked and greatly outnumbered, would certainly have retreated to the next good, defensive position and none could have blamed him. Instead, at midnight of April 30, he sent Major General Lafayette McLaws' Division to reinforce Anderson's thin line. Then, at dawn on May 1, Stonewall Jackson followed with three more divisions. That left Jubal Early with just one division (slightly reinforced) to try to hold Fredericksburg against Sedgwick and two Union corps. In the Confederate commander in chief's mind there does not seem to have been any thought of retreat. It was simply a question of which of the two Union attack groups he should engage. He chose to try to hold Fredericksburg with a very small force while concentrating the rest of his army against General Hooker's main thrust.

When General Jackson reached the line held by Anderson and McLaws he promptly ordered all entrenching to stop. The troops were to advance immediately and attack the Union army. When, shortly afterward, Lee reached the scene he immediately approved Jackson's decisions. This surprise attack against greatly superior numbers must have confused General Hooker. He was supposed to be advancing forward that day to annihilate the Confederate army and he now suddenly found himself attacked. He hastily ordered a retreat. The first definite signs of a lack of confidence in himself and his plans were showing. The Union generals were amazed, protested, but obeyed. The Confederates were just as surprised and moved forward slowly and carefully, fearing a trap. That night both sides entrenched where they stood.

That same night Lee and Jackson discussed the situation. Their forces were outnumbered but they had captured the initiative. They must retain it or eventually fall back before superior numbers. The decision reached at that historic conference was one of the great decisions of the war. No two commanders who were not supremely confident of each other's ability would have even suggested the plan; the risk was tremendous but the stakes were high. The small Confederate army would divide into two separate parts in the very face of the greatly superior foe. Jackson with his three divisions was to march around the right flank of the Union army and attack its right rear. Lee was to hold the present position with only two divisions, less than 20,000 men. He was to keep Hooker with four times that many, occupied; and then attack when Jackson did. If the attack on May 1 had been surprising, this was almost unbelievable. If Hooker ever discovered what Lee had done, where Jackson had gone, the result would be fatal to Lee's little force.

Early in the morning of May 2 Stonewall Jackson started his most famous march. Today, we can follow his trail, marked for us by the government, first south, then north to the Brock Road thence to Wilderness Corner on the Orange Turnpike, now State Highway 3. It was quite a long march and, of course, took considerable time. We can imagine Lee's feelings all that long day as he waited and waited, wondering if Hooker would discover the movement and attack. But Hooker never did. Instead of attacking, Hooker called for one of the two corps from Fredericksburg to come to his assistance. It was getting late in the day, would Jackson manage to get into position and attack before dark?

No one ever needed to tell Stonewall Jackson the value of time. He was saving every minute he could, yet making very sure that everything was in order. Here, as at Shiloh, we find the Confederates preparing to attack in line, division by division. An unusual method it was, but it saved precious seconds. As unit after unit reached the scene they were hurried into line, stretching across the road, through that forest of underbrush, second-growth oak and pine, called the Wilderness, so thick and so tangled with vines a soldier could not see more than a few yards ahead. Today in many places it is still the same dense, impenetrable scrubby forest, There are many more farms in the area now, but the woods, especially along the line of Jackson's march, still deserve that most appropriate name of the Wilderness.

At 5:15 p.m. General Jackson looked at his watch, then calmly gave the order to advance. Loud and clear through the Wilderness the Confederate bugles rang. The attack burst upon the Union army and rolled up the Union right. Lee was also attacking on his front. How far the Confederates could have gone we cannot say. Darkness came too soon for them that day, and with the darkness came tragedy for the Confederacy. General Stonewall Jackson, while on reconnaissance in front of his lines at dusk, was shot by accident by his own men. He died eight days later. The Confederacy paid dearly for the victory at Chancellorsville. Today, Jackson's battlefield monument stands beside the road near the Park Information Station on State Highway 3.

The next day the Confederates renewed their assaults. In the action of May 2 they had routed only a part of the Union army, most of it was still intact, but they had soundly whipped its commander. "Fighting Joe" Hooker's fighting spirit had definitely cooled. From then on he could think of nothing but holding his line or retreating. To make matters worse for the Union forces, a Confederate solid shot struck a pillar of the house he was using as his headquarters. A piece fell off and, temporarily, knocked him unconscious. He appeared to be in a daze for the rest of the day.

In the middle of the story of Chancellorsville we must turn to the Battles of Marye's Heights and Salem Church on the opposite flank near Fredericksburg. About midnight of May 2, the night of Jackson's attack, Sedgwick received an order from Hooker to advance through Fredericksburg toward the rear of Lee's army at Chancellorsville. Although Hooker had already that day taken from him one of his two corps, Sedgwick hastened to obey. At daybreak his troops assaulted Marye's Heights. Jubal Early's lone division repulsed attack after attack but the line was far too thin to hold indefinitely. About noon Sedgwick's men broke through and headed for Chancellorsville.

Late that afternoon Sedgwick reached the Salem Church, one of the principal landmarks of the battlefield, just south of the Orange Turnpike (State Highway 3). Here he ran into General McLaws' Confederate Division, sent by Lee from Chancellorsville to stop this new Union threat. The next day, May 4, Anderson's Division also arrived. Together with what was left of Early's troops they attacked, driving northward toward the river. That night Sedgwick escaped. General Lee then turned his army back toward Chancellorsville but Hooker did not wait for him. He also fled to safety across the river.

In the Campaign and Battle of Chancellorsville, including the Battles of Marye's Heights and Salem Chruch, the Union losses in killed, wounded, captured and missing totaled about 17,000 men. The Confederates lost about 13,000.

From Chancellorsville to
Vicksburg and Gettysburg

MAY 4, 1863, saw the Confederate Army of Northern Virginia victorious on the battlefield of Chancellorsville. By July 4, 1863, just two months later, the tide had turned. If anyone were asked to select the most decisive period of the war covering only a short span of time, he would probably select these two months.

In the West, the campaign and surrender of Vicksburg opened the Mississippi Valley to the Union, splitting the Confederacy in two. In the East, Lee's second invasion of the North ended in failure at Gettysburg. These two events establish this period as the turning point of the war, though the struggle was still to last two more long years.

In addition, we also find in this same period that the Union army at Murfreesboro finally advanced. Late in June, in a very short campaign lasting only a week General Rosecrans out-maneuvered General Bragg from his position at Tullahoma, forcing him to retreat south toward Chattanooga.

Farther to the west General Banks pushed up the Red River to capture Alexandria, Louisiana, then turned back to besiege Port Hudson on the Mississippi. The Confederates west of the river then directed their attention toward assisting the garrisons of Port Hudson and Vicksburg. In the month of June they recaptured some of the territory lost in southern Louisiana and advanced east to the Mississippi. This move served to frighten the Union forces at New Orleans but did not aid the Confederates trapped at Port Hudson.

In Arkansas the Confederates attacked Helena hoping to draw troops away from Vicksburg. The attack was repulsed but was, in any event, too late. It occurred on the very day that Vicksburg fell.

Before we turn to a description of the Vicksburg campaign it would be advisable, to avoid confusion, to note an interesting fact concerning the names of the various armies of the North and the South. The Union armies were usually given the names of rivers, whereas the Confederate armies were usually given territorial names. General Bragg's Confederate army at the battle of Murfreesboro was called the Army of Tennessee. In the campaign of Vicksburg we will find General Grant's Union army designated as the Army of the Tennessee. Other examples are the Union Army of the Cumberland, the Union Army of the Potomac and the Confederate Army of Northern Virginia. Later on, in the Atlanta campaign there will also be the Union Army of the Ohio and, in the East, the Union Army of the James.

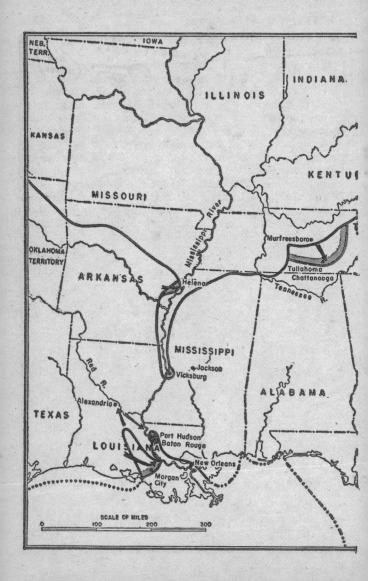

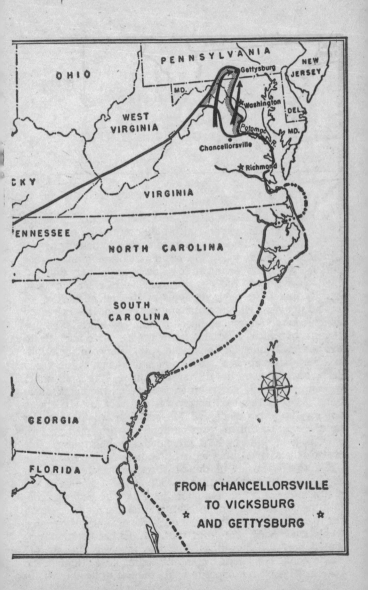

FROM CHANCELLORSVILLE
TO VICKSBURG
AND GETTYSBURG

The Campaign of Vicksburg

VICKSBURG was one of the great, fortified strongpoints of the Civil War. It stood on a high bluff overlooking the Mississippi River, its batteries ready to dispute the passage of any Union ship. Even today the position looks formidable but during the Civil War the river followed an entirely different channel. Right at the city it made a great hairpin bend directly under the menacing guns of the defenders.

The site was well chosen for another reason. It is extremely difficult for an army to approach it from the North. The line of hills, of which Vicksburg forms a part, turns abruptly to the northeast following the Yazoo River. Between these hills and the Mississippi is a vast bottom land known as the Yazoo delta, stretching northward for 175 miles. It is sixty miles wide in places, and covers an area of several thousand square miles. Most of this land is very soft and very low. If it were not for the levees along the Mississippi it would be under water a great part of the year. Crisscrossed with small streams, large bayous, and rivers, it presented an almost impassable obstacle to a large army with heavy guns and wagons.

On the other side of the Mississippi opposite Vicksburg the bottom land, though not as wide as the Yazoo delta, extends both north and south of the city. The problem confronting an army trying to capture Vicksburg was to reach the high ground east of the Yazoo River or south of the city, and assault Vicksburg from the rear. Either solution presented immense difficulties. The first involved crossing the Yazoo delta. The alternative meant finding a way through the bottom land on the opposite bank, then crossing the Mississippi to the eastern shore. Supply would be difficult in either case, perhaps impossible by the second method because the supply ships would have to run down past the Vicksburg batteries to reach the troops operating below the city.

As already described in the chapter "From Antietam to Fredericksburg and Murfreesboro," General Grant's first effort to capture Vicksburg by a combined land and water movement had failed. This had been in November and December of 1862. From then on the Union forces were based on the west side of the river opposite, but somewhat north of the city. For the next four months they tried various ways to cross the Yazoo delta or to by-pass the city. A total of four more unsuccessful attempts were to be made before the fifth finally succeeded and General Grant's Army of the Tennessee could engage the Confederate forces in open warfare.

Before describing the various efforts of the Union forces to reach Vicksburg it would help to set the scene by describing briefly the conditions under which the troops operated. It was wintertime, and this meant chilly, rainy weather. In such a low, swampy country it was almost impossible to find dry land. Everything—clothing, tents, bedding—was wet and stayed wet. Malarial fever and smallpox broke out among the troops. Yet the work went on under these terrible conditions, and most of it was just plain hard labor. This first phase of the campaign of Vicksburg was primarily an engineer's war of digging and construction rather than of combat.

Not only was this first phase an engineer's war but also a naval war. Every plan of approach to Vicksburg entailed movement over water, whether it was by river or through a bayou. In this campaign, General Grant was very fortunate in having assigned to work with him an extremely capable and energetic naval officer, Admiral David D. Porter. In fact, the army's efforts to reach the Confederate stronghold of Vicksburg would have been absolutely impossible without the help of the navy.

The four unsuccessful efforts to reach Vicksburg can be resolved into two attempts to by-pass the city to the south and two to cross the Yazoo delta to the north. At times, work on all four projects was carried on simultaneously. The first of these was the digging of a canal across the narrow neck of land opposite the city. This work was started prior

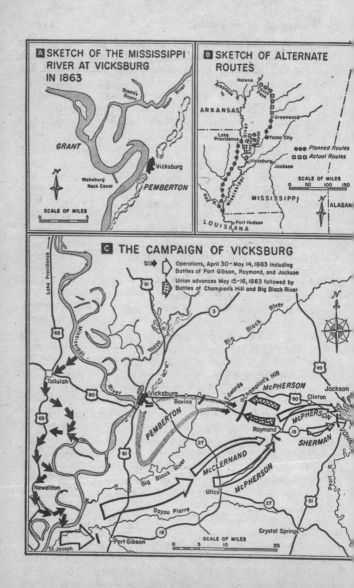

A SKETCH OF THE MISSISSIPPI RIVER AT VICKSBURG IN 1863

Steele's Bayou
Yazoo River
GRANT
Vicksburg
Vicksburg Neck Canal
PEMBERTON
N
SCALE OF MILES
0 5

B SKETCH OF ALTERNATE ROUTES

Arkansas
Helena
Yazoo Pass
ARKANSAS
Greenwood
Yazoo City
Lake Providence
Vicksburg
Jackson
MISSISSIPPI
ALABAMA
LOUISIANA
Port Hudson
●●● Planned Routes
□□□ Actual Routes
SCALE OF MILES
0 50 100 150
N

C THE CAMPAIGN OF VICKSBURG

➡ Operations, April 30 - May 14, 1863 including Battles of Port Gibson, Raymond, and Jackson

⬧ Union advances May 15-16, 1863 followed by Battles of Champion's Hill and Big Black River

Lake Providence
61
3
65
Tallulah
80
Yazoo
Big Black River
49
Vicksburg
Edwards
Champion's Hill
McPHERSON
Jackson
Bovina
80
Clinton
PEMBERTON
McPHERSON
65
61
Raymond
SHERMAN
Newellton
27
McCLERNAND
18
Big Black River
Mississippi River
Utica
McPHERSON
27
51
Pearl R.
Bayou Pierre
St. Joseph
Port Gibson
18
Crystal Springs
SCALE OF MILES
0 5 10 20
N

to General Grant's arrival and continued for two months thereafter. Although Grant, himself, did not have much hope for this solution, the President was anxious that the effort be made, so the work was pushed with vigor and determination. Much of the digging was done by hand, though dredges were also used. The attempt failed. The levee at the north end of the canal broke and the water poured in and flooded the whole Vicksburg Neck. Yet the dreary work went on until eventually Confederate artillery across the river, below the city, stopped the effort completely.

The other attempt to by-pass Vicksburg, known as the Lake Providence Route, was purely a construction project, and no Confederate opposition was ever encountered. The plan, in this instance, was to cut a canal from the Mississippi River into Lake Providence, then to pass through an intricate network of bayous and rivers for a distance of two hundred miles—south to the Red River. Counting the return passage up the Mississippi, this route would have meant a detour of nearly four hundred miles to reach Vicksburg from the south. This effort was abandoned when it was found that a special type of underwater saw would be needed to remove obstructions. Nearly two months of planning and hard work were also poured into this failure.

The two efforts to cross the delta provide a great deal more interest. The first of these, called the Yazoo Pass Route, appeared quite promising although it was very long and winding, stretching all the way from near Helena, Arkansas, to Yazoo City, Mississippi. The Confederates cut trees to fall across the water and clog the way for the gunboats and ironclads. It took a month for the Union navy to thread its way through this inland swamp to as far as Greenwood, Mississippi. Here the Confederates had constructed Fort Pemberton (named for the Confederate commander at Vicksburg, Lieutenant General John C. Pemberton). It was made of cotton bales and only mounted eight guns, but the surrounding country was under water. The Union army could not march on the land and the channel was so narrow that the gunboats could not maneuver. The expedition was forced to halt and then turn back.

The story of the Steele's Bayou Route is the most intriguing of all. It was attempted as a diversion to help the forces struggling through the Yazoo Pass Route. Admiral Porter himself commanded the naval force which led the way; General Sherman followed with parts of his corps. Almost immediately Admiral Porter ran into trouble. The passage which had been represented to him as comparatively simple was blocked by trees, some of them three feet in diameter. With his ironclads Porter knocked down the trees, pulled others up by the roots, tore his way through bridges, but at that rate found himself making only four miles a day. Then the flagship became stuck in a bed of willows. It took the combined efforts of all the other ships to pull it out. The Confederates closed in and began to fell trees in rear of the ships which could not turn around but had to back out. Sharpshooters lined the bank so that no one dared show himself on deck.

Admiral Porter's call for help reached General Sherman who hastily dispatched all the troops he had at hand. Then, alone in a canoe. Sherman paddled through the swampland to reach more Union soldiers and lead them forward that night through a dense canebrake by candlelight. He arrived just in time to save the Union fleet from capture by the Confederate army. It took four more days to disentangle the fleet. During the first three the ships were still backing out, looking for a place wide enough to turn around.

Every attempt to reach Vicksburg had failed. The Northern people, forgetting General Grant's victories at Fort Henry, Fort Donelson, and Shiloh, began to call for his removal. But in spite of the unfavorable criticism and the clamor in the public press, General Grant steadfastly refused to divulge his plans. To his eternal credit, President Lincoln stood behind his army commander, letting him work out his problem in his own way.

At this moment, Major General Ulysses S. Grant was certainly at the crossroads of his career. All those qualities for which he is so well remembered: persistence, calm determination, quiet resolution, relentless hammering at the enemy, had availed him nothing. The memory of his later campaign in the East and the final, long siege of Petersburg tend to make us think of those qualities alone and forget the daring and unorthodox way in which he finally did by-pass Vicksburg. Nor should we overlook the lightning campaign that followed, when in just eighteen days the Confederates were defeated in five separate battles, then bottled up in the city. These operations alone would establish beyond any doubt Grant's place in history as an outstanding general and leader.

His final plan was extremely hazardous. It was to march down the west bank of the Mississippi, cross the river below Vicksburg, and there, with only supplies that could be taken with the troops, abandon his line of communications and all hope of resupply in case of defeat. As soon as General Grant divulged his plan to Admiral Porter, that officer immediately agreed to do his part. But no one else was enthusiastic and even his trusted subordinate, General Sherman, argued against the plan as too great a gamble.

The movement began late in March. Using small boats and constructing roads, which promptly turned into seas of mud as they advanced, it took a month for the Union forces to wind their way across the bottom land opposite Vicksburg. Only two corps were employed in this movement, those of Major General McClernand and Major General McPherson. The other corps, commanded by Sherman, was temporarily left near Vicksburg to demonstrate against the city and confuse the Confederates as to Grant's intentions.

On the night of April 6, 1863, occurred one of the dramatic events of the war, the passage of the first part of the Union fleet past the Vicksburg batteries. Admiral Porter made his preparations with great care; the sides of the transports were piled high with cotton, hay and grain, and even the ironclads were strengthened with logs. But the Confederates were on the alert for just such an attempt. As the ships drifted down with the current, the defenders of Vicksburg lit huge barrels of tar and set fire to buildings to light the scene. For two and a half hours the bombardment lasted but only one transport was sunk. Six nights later the remainder of the fleet successfully ran the batteries. Admiral Porter was now safely below the city and ready to assist Grant's army across the river.

In the meantime, to further confuse the Confederate leaders, a large force of Union cavalry under the command of Colonel Benjamin H. Grierson, swept southward through Mississippi down into Louisiana, joining the Union forces in the southern part of that State. There was no Confederate cavalry on hand to oppose the move; all of it had been sent to Tennessee. The Union raid caused great alarm and excitement, diverting attention away from Grant's operations. For that reason alone, this raid is generally considered to be one of the most successful operations of the war.

On April 30 the Union forces started across the Mississippi. On this date General Grant's army, including Sherman's Corps still at Vicksburg, numbered about 50,000 men. The Confederate strength in the area was about 31,000, the greater part concentrated in or near the city. Only two brigades could be hastily assembled to oppose the crossing. These were decisively defeated at the Battle of Port Gibson on the following day. The Union forces then pushed forward to seize the ground to the east and there await the arrival of Sherman's Corps which reached the scene a week later.

During this period the Confederate commander, General Pemberton, should have been concentrating his forces. He sent some troops toward the Big Black River, but he left two divisions idle at Vicksburg. Furthermore, when some reinforcements intended for his army reached Jackson and Raymond farther to the east, he left them to guard that area. In effect, he strung his forces out on a line all the way from Vicksburg east to Jackson, far too large an area for his inferior numbers to hold.

Instead of moving north as General Pemberton expected him to do, General Grant turned northeast, completely abandoning his line of communications, depending upon the country to provide his supplies. His object was to place his army between Jackson and Vicksburg. By doing so he could cut the Confederate supply line into Vicksburg, stop reinforcements from reaching the city, and also stand squarely across Pemberton's probable line of retreat.

On May 12 the Union forces defeated a Confederate brigade at Raymond. The next day General Joseph E. Johnston arrived at Jackson to take command and found only two Confederate brigades present on the field. These were defeated the following day. General Grant then promptly turned toward Vicksburg. On May 16, he won a hard-fought battle at Champion's Hill, the decisive engagement of the campaign. The following day the Union forces forced a crossing of the Big Black River. By evening of May 18 they reached the outskirts of Vicksburg. President Lincoln's trust in General Grant had been fully justified.

The Siege of Vicksburg

As soon as he could possibly get his troops into position Grant ordered a general assault on Vicksburg. He hoped, by so doing, to take advantage of Confederate demoralization and disorganization after the retreat. The attack, delivered on May 19, failed. Three days later, still hoping that he could carry the works and finish the campaign without a long, drawn out siege, he ordered another assault. His troops, as anxious to end the fighting, and as confident as their commanding general, rushed forward to the attack. But Vicksburg was a naturally strong position surrounded by steep ravines, most difficult to climb. The defenders had further strengthened the natural defenses and were determined to hold them at all costs. At only one point, the Railroad Redoubt, was the actual line of fortifications breached, but the breach could not be maintained. Both sides settled down to a long siege.

In this assault of May 22 two separate attacks were made. General McClernand, by misleading reports, caused Grant to believe that his corps might be succeeding in its attack. McClernand requested the other corps to redouble their efforts. Although doubtful of his subordinate's claims, General Grant could not afford to ignore them if they were actually true. He ordered a second attack which also failed. This was just one of many counts in a long list of complaints against General McClernand, the same officer who, six months before, had tried by political skulduggery to have himself placed in command of the Vicksburg expedition. Since then there had been a number of just complaints against him. Most observers agree that the only criticism of General

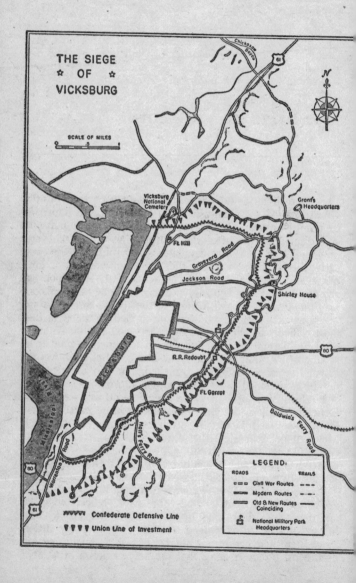

THE SIEGE
☆ OF ☆
VICKSBURG

SCALE OF MILES

Chickasaw Bayou

61

N

Vicksburg National Cemetery

Grant's Headquarters

Ft. Hill

Graveyard Road

Jackson Road

Shirley House

R.R. Redoubt

80

Ft. Garrot

Baldwin's Ferry Road

Hall's Ferry Road

Warrenton Road

80

61

wwww Confederate Defensive Line

▼▼▼▼ Union Line of Investment

LEGEND:

ROADS   TRAILS

▭▭▭ Civil War Routes   – – –

▬▬▬ Modern Routes   –·–·–

▬▬▬ Old & New Routes
        Coinciding

🏛   National Military Park
     Headquarters

Grant's conduct during this period is that he was too patient and forebearing. Perhaps he remembered McClernand's brave defense at Shiloh which had done so much to save the day.

Finally, however, General McClernand committed the unpardonable offense of publishing a congratulatory general order to his troops in which he slighted the efforts of the other corps. The order even criticized General Grant for not having done more to help the corps during the assault of the 22nd, which was, as we have seen, absurd. When this order was published in the newspapers and reached the army, Grant promptly relieved McClernand from command. His own corps, as well as the rest of the army, was glad to see him go.

As the siege progressed Genral Grant's army was reinforced until it reached a strength of over 70,000 men. Gradually the Union lines drew closer to the Confederate positions until they were within only a few yards in many places, close enough to throw hand grenades at each other. In this kind of warfare the Confederates were at a great disadvantage. They had none of their own and were forced to try to catch the Union grenades and throw them back before they exploded.

Although there was occasionally some fraternization at points along the line, the siege was for the most part a very grim business. The Union army and navy continuously, night and day, shelled Vicksburg. The civilian inhabitants hid in caves dug into the hills. The soldiers, rarely out of the trenches for even a few short mintues, fought on bravely but with little hope. Ammunition ran low, food became practically nonexistent. Yet day after day the Confederate guns still fired. Famous old Fort Hill, which had seen French, English, and Spanish flags flying over it, helped to sink a Union gunboat. Finally on the Fourth of July, a day never since celebrated in this city, Vicksburg capitulated. There never had been much hope that it could be saved. The defenders had held out as long as humanly possible but it was known that General Grant was planning an attack for July 6. The Confederates, worn out by fatigue and lack of food, could never have withstood the overpowering Union numbers. We can only admire them for holding out for so many weary weeks.

The Campaign of Gettysburg

AFTER the Battle of Chancellorsville and the death of Stonewall Jackson, the Army of Northern Virginia was reorganized into three corps. Lieutenant General James Longstreet retained command of the First Corps. Richard S. Ewell, although greatly handicapped by the loss of a leg at Groveton on the day preceding the Second Battle of Manassas, was appointed to command the Second Corps. Later, on the first day of the Battle of Gettysburg, he was to be hit again in the same leg. But, as he calmly announced, it didn't hurt at all to be shot in a wooden leg. The commander of the Third Corps was General A. P. Hill. Both Ewell and Hill were newly appointed lieutenant generals.

Lee's army was 70,000 strong. The officers and men were supremely confident of themselves and their commander. Most of them had been actively campaigning for two years and, during that time, had almost always defeated their more numerous opponents. Thoroughly trained in every phase of combat, completely inured to hard service in the field under all conditions, the Army of Northern Virginia constituted as fine a unit as ever went into battle. When General Lee decided to advance northward the army responded with alacrity.

Across the river from Fredericksburg the Union Army of the Potomac numbered over 100,000 men. Its commander was still the same General Hooker who had been at Chancellorsville. From his actions in that battle it was obvious that President Lincoln must choose another general before the army fought again, but he had not yet decided whom he should select. The army was organized into seven corps as it had been at Chancellorsville, but most of the units were understrength. The Union forces were plagued, as always, by the peculiar replacement system which brought new, untrained regiments to the army—but rarely filled the ranks of the veteran units. The latter were as capable and efficient as any troops the South could bring against them but the regiments too often numbered what battalions should.

Thoroughly aware of the conditions prevailing in both camps, General Lee embarked upon his second invasion of the North. The reasons for this decision were essentially the same as before; to gain foreign recognition of the Confederacy by a victory on Northern soil, and to induce the Northern peace party to stop the war. In addition, there was hope that the pressure on Vicksburg might be lessened. Further, the Confederate troops were badly in need of supplies which could probably be obtained in the North. In fact, the Battle of Gettysburg was actually precipitated by an expedition to the town to obtain shoes for the Southern soldiers.

The campaign actually began on June 3 when General Lee started to move toward Culpeper. One week later two of his three corps were concentrated there. On June 9 at Brandy Station occurred one of the most significant cavalry battles of the war because here, for the first time the Union horsemen held their own against the Confederates. They thereby gained that much-needed confidence in their ability which was essential if they were ever to perform their duties efficiently. Prior to this date the superiority of the Southern horsemen had been universally recognized. From now on the cavalry of the North fought on more equal terms.

For the march into Pennsylvania, General Lee divided his army into three parts. General Ewell's Corps led the way, followed by Longstreet and A. P. Hill. By the evening of June 13 Ewell had reached Winchester. In the next two days the second battle named for that city was fought. The Confederates captured 4000 prisoners and a large quantity of munitions including twenty-five cannon. General Ewell pressed vigorously forward toward the Potomac.

In the meantime General Hooker had asked permission of the authorities in Washington to attack the isolated Confederate corps at Fredericksburg and then march on Richmond. When his request was disapproved he withdrew from

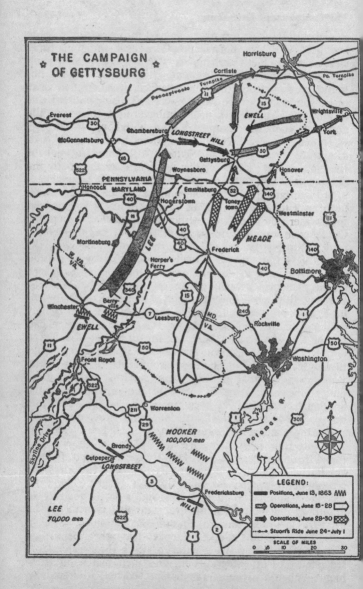

THE CAMPAIGN OF GETTYSBURG

LEGEND:
- Positions, June 13, 1863
- Operations, June 13-28
- Operations, June 28-30
- Stuart's Ride June 24-July 1

SCALE OF MILES
0   5   10   20   30

Fredericksburg. For the next two weeks his movements simply paralleled those of General Lee, Hooker keeping his army west of Washington and moving north as Lee marched up through Maryland and on into Pennsylvania.

Everything seemed to be going exactly according to Lee's plans. During these two weeks Ewell's Corps moved steadily forward through Pennsylvania. One column captured Carlisle and threatened Harrisburg. Another column passed through Gettysburg, captured York, and entered Wrightsville. Here a small force of Union militia set fire to the bridge across the river. In doing so they almost burned down the town; the advancing Confederates managed to save it from destruction.

But one fatal mistake had been made. Jeb Stuart, taking advantage of too general an order from Lee, had led his cavalry on another ride around the Union army and had not yet returned. Lee was operating without the eyes and ears of the army, without the information about enemy movements which only the cavalry in those days could bring. He did not know where Hooker's Union forces were, nor did he learn until June 28 that the Union army had crossed the Potomac two days before and also that a new general had been appointed by President Lincoln to lead it.

Major General George G. Meade was the new commander of the Army of the Potomac, a position he held until the end of the war. This time the President had made a fortunate selection. The new general promptly marched from Frederick, Maryland, toward Harrisburg, the better to cover the Baltimore-Washington area. Although he sent a cavalry division to make a reconnaissance to Gettysburg, this town was not his objective. He intended to concentrate his forces several miles to the southeast.

In the meantime General Lee hastily sent orders to his troops to concentrate west of Gettysburg. He still did not know where the Union army was as General Stuart had not yet rejoined him. In fact, Stuart did not return to Lee until the second day of the battle, and his cavalry was so exhausted that they could not be put into action until the third day. The supplies destroyed or captured by Stuart's Cavalry in this eastward raid in no way compensated for the handicap his absence imposed on his commander in chief.

On June 30 a Confederate brigade marched toward Gettysburg hoping to obtain some shoes stored there. Upon discovering the Union cavalry in possession of the town, they retired. On the following day the Confederates returned in greater strength. Thus neither army commander actually chose the battlefield. Each was trying to concentrate on opposite sides of the town, several miles apart from each other. The selection of the site for the greatest battle ever fought on the American continent was an accident.

The Battle of Gettysburg

On July 1, 1863, the town of Gettysburg was occupied by two brigades of Brigadier General John Buford's First Cavalry Division. Although there had been some skirmishing with Confederate infantry on the preceding day, this was not unusual. Many such small actions had occurred ever since the beginning of the campaign. There was no reason whatever to believe that anything of national importance would ever occur here. Gettysburg was just another place on the map of Pennsylvania.

A closer look at the map would have revealed the fact that Gettysburg was the center point of a number of roads radiating north, south, east, and west. The town itself had no military significance, but so many roads coming together here made it almost certain that units of one or perhaps both armies would pass this way during the course of the campaign. This had already happened. Only a few days before a Confederate column had passed through marching northeast on the York Pike (U.S. Highway 30). Now the Union forces occupied it, and a Confederate corps was approaching from the west.

The leading division, under Major General Henry Heth, approached slowly and carefully on the Chambersburg Pike (also U.S. Highway 30—on the west side of the town) with two brigades in front, one on each side of the road. They knew that Union forces occupied the town but that was all the information they had. It was actually a reconnaissance in force to develop the Union strength. They were met at first only by Buford's cavalrymen who gave ground slowly, contesting every foot of the way, hoping to last until the arrival of the Union infantry. For General Buford had seen for himself and appreciated the defensive possibilities of the ground around Gettysburg, and had called for assistance. Now it was his duty to hold the ground as long as possible.

Among the first to reach the scene was Major General John F. Reynolds, commander of the First Union Corps. Immediately following him came two infantry brigades, one of them the famous "Iron Brigade," perhaps the best known in the Army of the Potomac. One of the "Iron Brigade's" peculiarities was that they insisted on wearing the same old black hats which they had worn when first mustered into service. Seeing them, the Confederates knew immediately that they were facing more than Buford's cavalry. Now it was the Union army's turn to attack. The morning of July 1 ended with the Confederate advance firmly repulsed; unfortunately for the Union cause, General Reynolds was killed early in the action. He had been one of the most capable and at the same time one of the best-liked officers in the Army. The command of the Union troops was assumed, temporarily, by Major General Abner Doubleday, later to become famous as the founder of that most popular game—baseball.

No description of the Battle of Gettysburg would be complete if it did not include some of the stories or legends that have since arisen concerning this most famous battle fought on American soil. One of the best known is that of Gettysburg's town constable, old John Burns, a veteran of the war of 1812. Incensed at the invasion of his native soil, he marched off to join the Union forces. Though over seventy years old, he fought in the Union ranks this first day and was wounded three times.

The battle near Gettysburg was now attracting troops in great numbers. The remainder of the Union First Corps and then the Eleventh Corps arrived. Major General O. O. Howard, the senior officer on the field, assumed command. It is interesting to note that these troops came from the south. The normal situation was reversed. Confederate reinforcements were at the same time coming from the northeast and northwest, and they were arriving in greater numbers. Two divisions of General Ewell's Corps and two divisions of General A. P. Hill's Corps were now present, outnumbering the Union forces three to two.

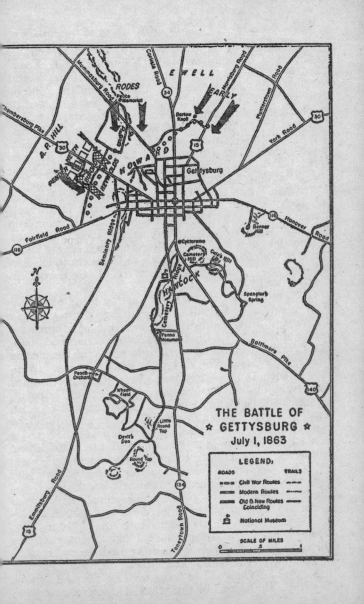

THE BATTLE OF
☆ GETTYSBURG ☆
July 1, 1863

LEGEND:

ROADS   TRAILS

▪▬ ▬ ▪ Civil War Routes ▬ ▬ ▬

▬ ▬ Modern Routes ▬ ▬ ▬

▬▬ Old & New Routes ▬▬▬
   Coinciding

🏛 National Museum

SCALE OF MILES

0   .5

The first assault of the afternoon was launched on the northwest of the town by Major General Robert E. Rodes' Division of Ewell's Corps from the vicinity of the present location of the Peace Memorial, dedicated on the 75th anniversary of the battle. At this point there was a sharp angle in the Union line and, furthermore, there was a gap in that line to the right. Nevertheless the Union troops held firmly, stoutly disputing possession of the ground, until Ewell's other division under Jubal Early attacked and captured Barlow Knoll, turning the Union right flank. About the same time General Heth renewed his assault on the Union left. When that officer was wounded in the head (he was probably saved from death by some paper in his hat), General Hill ordered Major General Pender's Division into the fray. With their right flank already turned, the combined weight of these divisions proved too great for the Union forces to withstand. They fled back to Cemetery Ridge leaving Seminary Ridge and the town of Gettysburg in Confederate hands.

One of the most famous stories of the battle of Gettysburg originated as a result of General Early's attack on the Union right flank, the decisive action of the day. During the course of this attack a Confederate brigade commander, General John B. Gordon, had particularly noted the outstanding bravery of a Union officer who was trying unsuccessfully to rally his men. Later when he rode forward, Gordon discovered him lying on the ground, severely wounded. Dismounting, he knelt beside him and asked if he could be of assistance. The Union officer, General Barlow, first said there was nothing that could be done, then asked if he could send a message to his wife who was supposed to be somewhere within the Union lines. Both men were sure that Barlow was dying but Gordon did send a man under a flag of truce with a message for Mrs. Barlow. At considerable risk of her own life she hurried to her husband's side. Eventually he recovered to read in the newspapers of the death in battle of a General J. B. Gordon of the Confederate Army. Naturally he assumed that it was the same man. Nearly fifteen years later the two men, each believing the other dead, were introduced in Washington and became firm friends.

Meanwhile, General Lee had arrived on the field in time to witness the success of this attack. He sent a message to

General Ewell to press forward and take Cemetery Hill, if practicable. About the same time Major General Winfield Scott Hancock, whose very presence always inspired confidence, arrived to take command of the Union forces. He immediately started to organize the defense on a new line southeast of Gettysburg. General Ewell, after studying the situation, decided that it was not practicable to assault this strong position on Cemetery Hill. Almost every military historian has now agreed that this decision was a mistake, that the position could have been carried that evening.

July 2nd: It was General Lee's intention, expressed the evening before, to attack early in the morning of the second day. All but one infantry division of the Confederate army had either reached the field or was within a short distance. General Meade had arrived about 1:00 a.m. but, by 7:00 a.m., he still had with him on the ground only three-fourths of his command. The leading elements of his last corps did not arrive until about 2:00 p.m., after a gruelling march of thirty-four miles, with the men almost exhausted. Time was obviously on the Union side. However, the Confederate attack did not begin until late in the afternoon.

Part of this time was undoubtedly consumed in deciding exactly where the assault should be made. Cemetery Ridge is a long low ridge dominated at each end by hills. To the north are Cemetery Hill and Culp's Hill. To the south are the Round Tops. If the Confederates could secure any of these the Northern troops would be forced to retreat. The best chance to take Cemetery Hill had been lost the evening before. Therefore General Lee decided to have Longstreet make the main attack against the Union left with the divisions of Hood, McLaws, and Anderson. Simultaneously, General Ewell was supposed again to attack the hills on the Union right.

Longstreet was very slow in moving. He did not believe in the wisdom of Lee's plan and was extremely reluctant to execute it. In addition, some time was lost trying to find a route by which the troops could get into position without being observed. In this effort they were not entirely successful for a peculiar reason, which was to have a great bearing on the coming day's battle.

General Meade had ordered that the left of the Union line

be placed along Cemetery Ridge. But the corps commander, Major General Daniel E. Sickles, thought that some slightly higher ground about a mile to his front would be a better position. He sent some scouts forward to the Peach Orchard and it was these men who spotted Longstreet's column. Sickles then decided on his own initiative to move his line forward, without waiting for the commanding general's permission. This decision was almost fatal for, when the Confederate advance did come, his men were caught in a terribly exposed position, a mile in front of the rest of the line.

Longstreet finally attacked sometime after four o'clock in the afternoon. The assault was poorly coordinated. First came Hood's Division sweeping across the Devil's Den toward Little Round Top. At this crucial moment Major General Gouverneur K. Warren, the Chief Engineer of the Union army, on an inspection trip of the front line, discovered that there were no Union troops on Little Round Top, a position that must be held at all costs. General Hood's Confederates were charging forward to capture it and there was absolutely no one to stop them. Hastily Warren galloped for help. Some troops of Major General Sykes' Fifth Corps were moving forward to reinforce the exposed position at the Peach Orchard. These were diverted barely in time to save Little Round Top from capture, although the struggle was desperate and prolonged.

The battle spread to the north as McLaws attacked, followed by Anderson's men. The lines surged back and forth for hours through the Peach Orchard and the nearby Wheatfield. The Union troops, although reinforced by men from Sykes' and Hancock's Corps, were forced back after fierce fighting—but the Confederates could not capture Cemetery Ridge. It was here that the 1st Minnesota Infantry made its famous charge. It was one of those veteran Union regiments whose numbers had been so depleted by previous campaigns that its strength was less than a battalion. It was ordered to charge to plug a gap in the line, to charge against overwhelming numbers—the regiment did not hesitate. In a matter of minutes over eighty per cent of the men were dead or wounded but they had done their duty. They had plugged the gap in the line for long enough. There is no other unit in the history of warfare that ever made such a charge and then stood its ground sustaining such losses.

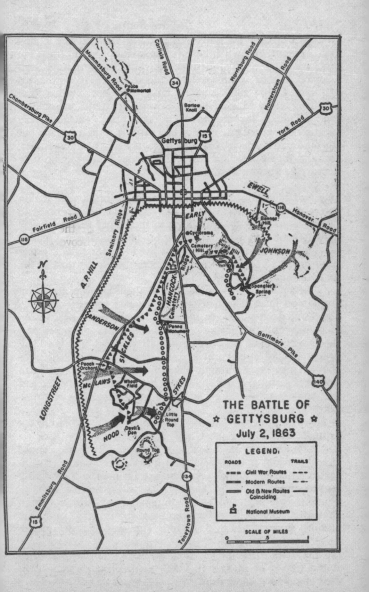

THE BATTLE OF
☆ GETTYSBURG ☆
July 2, 1863

LEGEND:

ROADS		TRAILS
— — —	Civil War Routes	– – –
— — —	Modern Routes	
————	Old & New Routes Coinciding	

National Museum

General Ewell was supposed to have attacked the Union right concurrently with Longstreet's assault. He did open fire with his artillery from Benner Hill but his guns were soon silenced. About sundown he made a rather uncoordinated attack on Culp's and Cemetery Hills. Only one division, that commanded by Major General Edward Johnson, was able to take and hold any ground. This ended the fighting of the second day. The Confederates had made a series of brave but uncoordinated attacks, first Hood, then McLaws, then Anderson and finally Ewell. They had gained ground but nothing decisive had been accomplished.

July 3rd: The third day's battle began at daybreak. The Union forces could not afford to let the Confederates continue to occupy a position so threatening to their right rear. In a very violent action in which the greater part of Major General Slocum's Twelfth Corps was involved the Southern forces were finally forced to withdraw. There was then a lull in the battle until afternoon.

General Lee was planning to make still another attack on the Union lines. The first day's battle had been favorable to the Confederates and, furthermore, they should have taken Cemetery Hill that evening. As for the results of the second day, General Lee knew that the attacks had not been coordinated and apparently believed that they had failed for that reason. It is certainly probable that if they had been delivered simultaneously, and early in the morning, as Lee had originally planned, the Confederates might have won this battle.

He therefore resolved to deliver a concentrated, fully coordinated assault on the Union center. As we look back on this decision with all the advantages of hindsight we cannot help but wonder if General Lee had not become overly infected with the supreme confidence of his men in their ability to accomplish anything. Certainly, by now, the Union position was well organized. It was quite a different situation from that which prevailed on the evening of the first day, or on the second day when Little Round Top was entirely unprotected.

The attack, to be preceded by an intense artilley bombardment, was to be made by 15,000 men. Although more than half of the men came from A. P. Hill's Corps, Longstreet was

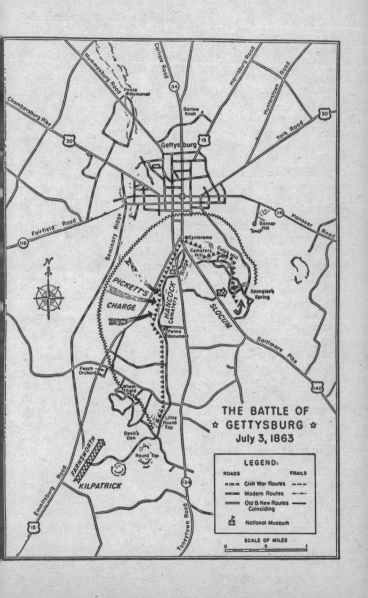

THE BATTLE OF
☆ GETTYSBURG ☆
July 3, 1863

LEGEND:

ROADS		TRAILS
▬▬▬ Civil War Routes		▬ ▬ ▬
▬▬▬ Modern Routes		
▬▬▬ Old & New Routes Coinciding		
⌂ National Museum		

SCALE OF MILES

0   ½   1

the senior corps commander and was therefore placed in charge. Only one of his divisions took part, Major General George E. Pickett's, which had not yet been engaged in the battle.

As on the preceding day, General Longstreet did not believe that his commanding general had made the correct decision. He was again slow in executing his orders; the artillery preparation did not begin until 1:00 p.m. Then the Union batteries joined in and there ensued a tremendous artillery duel, literally shaking the earth. At the word of command the 15,000 advanced as if on parade. There was a half mile of open, almost level, ground between the lines to cross, yet these men did not flinch though shot and shell tore through their ranks. "Pickett's Charge" has become synonymous with bravery. Only a few men managed to reach the Union line; they captured a short stretch, but could not hold it.

That same afternoon the Union and Confederate cavalry engaged in a battle, several miles east of the town, in which the Confederates were defeated. The final action of the battle was a cavalry charge, executed under protest, by Brigadier General E. J. Farnsworth against the right rear of the Confederate line. The Confederate infantry repulsed this useless charge with ease. Farnsworth and many of his men were killed.

The Union forces engaged in the Battle of Gettysburg numbered about 85,000. The Confederate army had from 70,000 to 75,000 men on the field. The casualties suffered by each side were also fairly equal. Union losses in killed, wounded, captured, and missing totaled a little over 23,000. The Confederates suffered something over 20,000 casualties but they could not replace them. The manpower of the South was almost exhausted.

From Vicksburg and Gettysburg
to the Battles around Chattanooga

On July 4, 1863, the same day that Vicksburg fell, General Lee began his retreat from Gettysburg. General Meade followed, but his pursuit was not conducted very vigorously. Ten days later the Confederate army was safely over the Potomac River. General Meade also crossed but for several weeks no more campaigning occurred. During the fall of the year the two armies maneuvered back and forth over northern Virginia, doing little damage to each other, and finally both went into winter quarters.

While General Grant had been besieging Vicksburg, a Confederate army had been collecting at Jackson, Mississippi, with the vain hope that it might be able to raise the siege. So long as Vicksburg held out, Grant could do nothing about this threat but on the very day of the surrender he dispatched General Sherman toward Jackson. The Confederates prudently retreated.

Port Hudson fell five days after Vicksburg. The Mississippi River was finally open to Union shipping. One of the major objectives of the Federal government had at last been accomplished. The Northern forces in the West could now turn toward other targets. General Grant was directed to transfer some of his troops to east Tennessee. Others were sent down the Mississippi to take part in an expedition into Texas. Several thousand were sent into Arkansas. In September, 1863, Fort Smith and Little Rock were captured. Union troops advanced as far south as Arkadelphia.

One of the boldest and most audacious cavalry raids of the war was undertaken during this period. Early in July, Brigadier General John H. Morgan rode into Kentucky with about 2500 soldiers and then, contrary to his orders, crossed the Ohio River near Louisville. From there he marched rapidly toward Cincinnati. The whole countryside was alerted. Hotly pursued, he swung south through Ohio toward the river, where he was attacked and most of his command captured. With a few men he fled northward but was soon forced to surrender near the Pennsylvania border. Several months later he escaped from prison and rejoined the Confederate army.

While General Morgan was engaged upon his fruitless Ohio raid, the Union army and navy began a quite different type of operation on the South Carolina coast. Army troops were landed on the beach near Fort Wagner. During July, aided by powerful naval gunfire, they launched two attacks on the fort. Both were hurled back with heavy losses. The Union forces began a regular siege, bombarding not only Fort Wagner but also Fort Sumter. In early September, Fort Wagner was evacuated but the Confederates clung stubbornly to Sumter, although its artillery power had been completely destroyed. A surprise attack by a boat party failed; this ended the efforts of the navy. The Union army continued its bombardment intermittently for months but Sumter remained in Confederate hands.

Although the attack on Fort Sumter occupied the attention of a number of ships of the Union navy for several months it did not result in any relaxation of the blockade. The stranglehold on the Atlantic and Gulf ports grew tighter with the passing of every month. Now, with the opening of the Mississippi River, the eastern half of the Confederacy was virtually surrounded. The problem was how to crack the hard core of Southern resistance. The section from Richmond, Virginia, south to Alabama was truly the hard central core, for in this area were located the factories, powder mills, and blast furnaces of the Confederacy. Destroy the munitions plants and the South would collapse.

The attention of both Union and Confederate generals automatically focussed upon Tennessee, and specifically upon Chattanooga, as the obvious gateway to this region. Just south of the city there was a gap in the mountain barrier and, in addition, Chattanooga was on the main East-West railroad line. The Civil War was the first large-scale war in which railroads played an important part. In the very first battle the Confederates had used them to concentrate their forces. In the final siege at Petersburg the cutting of Lee's railroad supply lines was a prime objective of Grant's army. In the forthcoming campaign of Chickamauga the railroads were to play a particularly outstanding part. A successful Union advance to, and beyond, Chattanooga would not only lead into the all-important munitions area but would also sever a vital railroad supply line connecting the East with the West.

In addition to Chattanooga, President Lincoln's attention was also directed toward Knoxville in east Tennessee. This city was also on the main East-West railroad but, far more important to the President, the people in this region were loyal to the North. He had been striving for two years to aid them. In preparation for this movement General Burnside had, for many months, been organizing and training the Army of the Ohio. In mid-August he moved forward, bypassing Cumberland Gap, and occupied the city practically without opposition. Five days later he captured the Confederate force at Cumberland Gap.

It seems surprising that east Tennessee, which had held out for so long against the Union armies, could be occupied so easily. There had been a Confederate corps at Knoxville under the command of Major General Buckner (the same officer who had surrendered at Fort Donelson but had been exchanged in a trade of prisoners of war). But this corps had been withdrawn for the defense of Chattanooga before Burnside arrived. The Confederates foresaw that the main battles would occur in that area and wanted everything concentrated there. A victory near Chattanooga would more than compensate for the loss of Knoxville. The real surprise was to come later when the Confederates violated this fundamental principle and detached a corps from Chattanooga at a most crucial stage in the operations. At the end of this period Burnside was to find himself besieged in Knoxville, the city he had so recently captured.

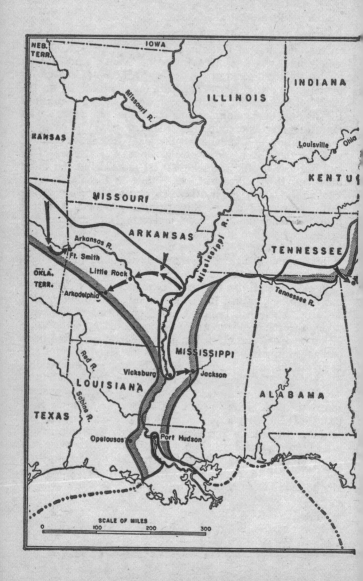

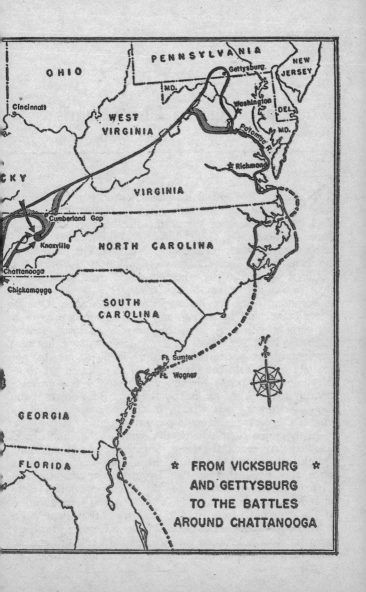

FROM VICKSBURG
AND GETTYSBURG
TO THE BATTLES
AROUND CHATTANOOGA

The Campaign of Chickamauga

ON August 16 General Rosecrans moved his army southward in several columns toward the Tennessee River. Four days later they reached the north bank near Stevenson, Alabama. By September 4, they were across the river and marching toward Chattanooga and North Georgia. The plan was to get behind the Confederate army, cut off its supplies, and bottle it up in the city where it would then be forced to fight its way out, surrender, or starve.

Accurately divining his opponent's intentions, General Bragg evacuated Chattanooga and moved southward to await his advance. Misinterpreting this move as a retreat, General Rosecrans hastily pushed his army forward as if he were conducting the pursuit of an enemy in flight. He did not hesitate to separate the Union forces in order to get them forward rapidly across the mountains on the few available country roads. This was exactly the right thing to do if the Confederate army was actually fleeing southward, but if by chance they were not, it could prove fatal.

In its march to this battle the Army of the Cumberland adopted very much the same formation that it had in its march to Murfreesboro. The Right, Center, and Left Wings were now designated as the Twentieth, Fourteenth, and Twenty-first Corps but they had the same commanders (Generals McCook, Thomas, and Crittenden) and were arranged in the same order from right to left. In addition, there was a reserve corps under Major General Gordon Granger. But there were forty miles between the left and right column, and no good connecting roads by which the troops could be assembled quickly for battle. If any one of the corps were attacked by the Army of Tennessee, the other corps could never come to its assistance in time.

Waiting and hoping for just such an opportunity to attack and overwhelm the Union corps individually while they were widely spread, General Bragg concentrated the Army of Tennessee near LaFayette, Georgia. Now, however, there were more Confederate troops on hand than there had been at Murfreesboro. Before the campaign opened Bragg had received reinforcements from Mississippi and he had also pulled General Buckner's corps in from Knoxville. His army was almost three times as strong as any one of the Union corps. With a naturally aggressive general like Braxton Bragg, history should have recorded the complete elimination of at least one Union corps, yet it did not.

It appears that General Bragg was not much better informed of the actual situation than General Rosecrans had been when he had made the mistake of dividing his army into three columns. General Bragg knew of the existence of two of them, the Union center and left, but probably was not even aware of the position of the third. If he did know of its existence he probably assumed that it was only a small, detached force, not of any great consequence. Therefore, thinking that the Northern troops were divided into two parts, he first aimed a blow at the leading division of the center corps, then turned to strike the Union left corps. though well conceived, both efforts failed. Neither attack was ever launched. The orders were issued but not executed. General Bragg was having his usual difficulties with his subordinates. The mutual trust and confidence, so necessary to military operations, were almost nonexistent.

Meanwhile, Rosecrans awoke to the fact that his enemy was not fleeing south, realized the dangerous position in which his army had been placed, and issued orders to bring them together. But it would take days, not hours, to accomplish this. Even after two of the columns joined, the Union troops would still be heavily outnumbered. All three corps were needed to face the entire Confederate army. Would Bragg wait that long before attacking?

It was not like Braxton Bragg to wait to attack, but he did. Before we criticize him too severely though, we should look at his side of the picture. He planned, correctly, to attack

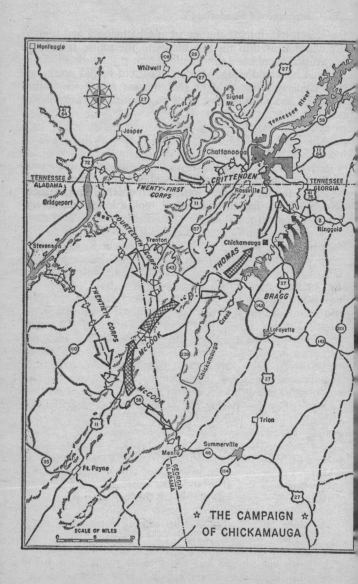

THE CAMPAIGN OF CHICKAMAUGA

the Union left, forcing it away from Chattanooga and rolling the whole army into the mountains to the south. If he had known that there was a third Union corps still far distant from the field he would surely have attacked, but he did not know this. General Bragg thought that he was facing the entire Army of the Cumberland and he wanted every available man on the ground for his attack. Several days before, the Confederate authorities in Richmond had dispatched a large part of Longstreet's Corps to his aid. Unfortunately, they had not yet arrived. The capture of Knoxville had cut the direct line from Richmond so that the Virginia troops had to come through the Carolinas and Georgia. The railroad system of the Confederacy was so overburdened and in such poor condition that the movement took a long time. Every conceivable type of rolling stock was used: boxcars, coal cars, and flatcars on which each man slept crosswise, rolled in a blanket. This was the longest Confederate troop movement by rail during the entire war.

How long could Bragg afford to wait? The longer he waited the more troops he would have but every day that he waited, his chances of success grew smaller and smaller. General Bragg chose a middle course. He waited until the first three brigades of Longstreet's Corps arrived on September 18, then ordered the attack. Some forward progress was made on that day but the actual battle did not begin until the following morning.

The Battle of Chickamauga

IN order to attack the Union army and carry out the plan of enveloping its left flank, the Confederates first had to cross Chickamauga Creek. In attempting to do so, they had found a number of the bridges and fords strongly defended. By evening of September 18 only a few units had reached the west bank. During the night there was considerable movement by the troops of both armies. The Confederates took advantage of the hours of darkness to push across the stream at various places. By daybreak of September 19 about three-fourths of Bragg's army was west of the creek.

At the same time the Union forces were also moving to protect their left flank. General Thomas' Corps, which had been in the center, moved over to the left, extending the Union lines much farther to the north. When morning came the Confederates were surprised to find that they were faced by far more troops than they had expected. As a matter of fact, it is doubtful if anyone on either side knew what to expect at daybreak on September 19. The battlefield of Chickamauga, which is being kept in approximately its wartime condition, is very densely wooded. After long night marches over unfamiliar territory where landmarks were practically nonexistent and every tree looked just like the last one, it is doubtful if anyone had a very clear conception of where his own units were, much less those of the enemy. The front lines stretched about six miles through the woods. An excellent view of the terrain, typical of this region, can be obtained from the Wilder Tower near the south end of the battlefield.

The fighting of September 19 was bitter, prolonged, and inconclusive. As brigade after brigade entered the fray all along the line, first one side then the other would attack or be attacked. During the afternoon the third Union corps arrived. Other Confederate troops crossed the creek to join in the battle. Before the day ended almost every unit of both armies had been engaged, yet neither side had made any substantial progress.

That night Lieutenant General Longstreet arrived with two more of the Virginia brigades. There was no one to meet him, and so he started with his staff to find General Bragg. Quite naturally, he lost his way in the woods. When he asked some soldiers what units they belonged to, they answered promptly with numerical designations. This was enough for General Longstreet; he quietly disappeared in the dark. The Union army numbered their units as we do in the United States Army today. The Confederates usually designated their by their commanders' names. Eventually General Longstreet arrived safely at Bragg's headquarters.

For the attack of September 20 General Bragg organized the Confederate forces into two parts. He placed the right half under the command of Lieutenant General Polk with orders to carry out the original plan of enveloping the Union left and roll the whole army back up into the mountains to the south. Longstreet was given command of the left half with orders to follow up Polk's assault.

When the Confederates advanced again to attack on the second day they found that the Union forces were not where they had been on the previous day. They had retreated slightly to a position more suited to defense and, at the same time, had shortened their lines, concentrating most of their strength against the very point where the Confederates were attacking. Even when led by such energetic commanders as Cleburne and Breckinridge, the Confederates made practically no progress at all. Bragg's plan of enveloping the Union left was not producing results. In spite of this the Southern troops continued their attacks, following the orders of their commander who had specified that the attack would begin on the right and be taken up progressively by each unit to its left along the whole line.

Polk's men had tried; now it was Longstreet's turn. His troops advanced to find suddenly a huge gap (where the

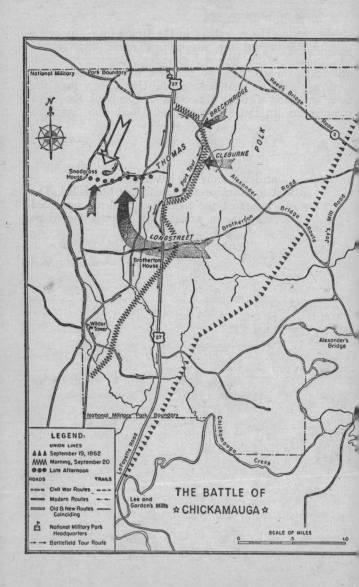

LEGEND:

UNION LINES
▲▲▲ September 19, 1862
〰〰 Morning, September 20
●●● Late Afternoon

ROADS   TRAILS
▬ ▬ Civil War Routes ▬ ▬
▬▬▬ Modern Routes ▬▬▬
▬▬▬ Old & New Routes ▬▬▬
    Coinciding

⌂   National Military Park
     Headquarters
→   Battlefield Tour Route

National Military Park Boundary
27
BRECKINRIDGE
Reed's Bridge
Road
2
THOMAS
Park Tour
CLEBURNE
POLK
Snodgrass
House
Alexander   Road
Joy's Mill Road
Bridge Route
LONGSTREET
Brotherton
Brotherton
House
Wilder
Tower
27
Alexander's
Bridge
National Military Park Boundary
Lafayette Road
Chickamauga
Creek
Lee and
Gordon's Mills

THE BATTLE OF
☆ CHICKAMAUGA ☆

SCALE OF MILES
0   .5   1.0

old Brotherton House stands) in the Union line. Through a misunderstanding of the situation, a whole division had left its place in the line and moved to reinforce the hard-pressed Union left. Through this hole the attackers poured, to drive the entire right flank of the Union army from the field, including General Rosecrans and two of the corps commanders. In this attack General Hood who had been severely wounded at Gettysburg (he went into this battle with a withered arm in a sling) lost his leg. That would have finished almost anyone else, but not General Hood. We shall see him again occupying an even more important position in the Confederate army at a later date.

The attempt to envelope the Union left had failed. The secondary attack against the right had suddenly succeeded beyond all expectation. In a matter of minutes the whole battle had been changed. Longstreet recognized this immediately and, contrary to his orders which had been to keep to his left, turned right to attack the remainder of the Union army.

This sudden change of direction by Longstreet almost finished the battle completely. The Union troops to his front had hastily formed a new line on the ridge just south of the Snodgrass House. Up this Longstreet's men surged. Victory seemed assured. At this opportune moment the First Division of Granger's Reserve Corps appeared and drove the attackers back again.

It was now the middle of the afternoon. There was plenty of time for the Confederates to reinforce their left where they were winning. Though Longstreet urged him to do so, General Bragg stubbornly insisted on trying to follow the original plan. As a result both halves of the Confederate Army continued to attack separately, uncoordinated in their efforts. Their attacks gradually gained ground but they were facing a very stubborn opponent.

What was left of the Union army was now under the command of Major General George H. Thomas, a former lieutenant in Bragg's battery during the Mexican War. Various assorted elements of all three corps, totaling approximately three-fourths of the entire Army of the Cumberland, were still on the field. George Thomas was a stubborn, patient man. He was slow to act, methodical, careful—not the type of man to be driven easily from a battlefield he had determined to hold.

At Murfreesboro he had held the center of the last Union line. Here on this field, he gained the name "The Rock of Chickamauga." His lines held until almost dark when he was forced back, still fighting stubbornly. Halfway to Chattanooga, Thomas found a new position and waited for a day but there was no pursuit. He then marched into the city.

It is quite difficult to state accurately either the forces engaged at Chickamauga or the losses sustained by each side. Estimates of both the Union and Confederate armies vary considerably. It is probable that the Union army had almost 60,000 men on the field against a Confederate strength of about 66,000 men. The Union losses were approximately 16,000 while the Confederates sustained about 18,000 casualties. In addition to having won the battle, the Confederates captured thousands of small arms and fifty-one guns. This victory, less than three months after the bitter defeats at Vicksburg and Gettysburg, gave new hope to the people of the South.

The Battles around Chattanooga

On December 31, 1862, the Army of Tennessee won a battle at Murfreesboro and then retreated, handing the city to the North. On September 20, 1863, the Army of Tennessee won another and greater victory at Chickamauga. Again, but on a grander scale, the results of that battle were thrown away.

The Union army retreated to Chattanooga. A few days later General Bragg laid siege to the city, hoping to starve out his enemy. If he had conducted a vigorous pursuit immediately after the Battle of Chickamauga he might have destroyed the Union army. By waiting, he gave them time to reorganize. The few hours lost before the Confederates moved forward were sufficient for the Union soldiers to entrench their position. Even after his failure to pursue, General Bragg could still have taken positive action to capitalize upon the results of his victory. A forward movement across the Tennessee River would have soon forced the Union army out of Chattanooga. Once in the open it might have been brought to battle again before reinforcements arrived. This great opportunity was lost. Instead, General Bragg decided to try siege methods.

Chattanooga, located on the banks of the Tennessee River, is almost entirely surrounded by high mountains. Today there are many main highways connecting the city with other localities to the north, south, east, and west. During the Civil War, however, the roads were not as numerous, and certainly not in good condition. Counting on this fact, General Bragg assumed that if he invested the south side of the

169

river and prevented supplies from reaching the Union troops by water or by the main highway from the west, the Union army would be forced to retreat or starved into surrender.

Confederate troops occupied Lookout Mountain, southwest of the city, a commanding position affording a magnificent view of the river where it makes a huge U-shaped bend. Possession of this mountain made it impossible for the Union army to receive supplies directly by water or by the main supply route, the road leading around the north end of Lookout Mountain. The besieging troops also occupied Missionary Ridge, southeast of the city, and likewise the valley between these two prominent mountain ranges. With this incomplete line, investing only the southern half of the city, General Bragg awaited developments.

Meanwhile the Confederate army was again having command difficulties. Bragg's generals came as close to open revolt against him as it was possible for them, as officers and gentlemen, to do. President Davis came west himself to try to settle the difficulties but failed to take the only possible action that could have solved the problem, i.e. to remove General Bragg. The Army of Tennessee would have to fight another battle, and lose it, before it received a commander worthy of itself.

For many weeks the Confederates faced Chattanooga while the North rushed reinforcements to Rosecrans. On October first Bragg sent General Joe Wheeler on a cavalry raid into Tennessee which caused a great deal of damage to the Union supply line north of the city. Except for this one venture, however, the Confederates did nothing but wait and see what Rosecrans might decide to do.

Actually, Rosecrans himself did nothing, but others in the North were busy on his behalf. "Fighting Joe" Hooker was hastily dispatched by rail from Virginia with parts of the Eleventh and Twelfth Corps of the Army of the Potomac. General Sherman started from the Mississippi with a large force from the Union Army of the Tennessee. Finally, almost a month after the battle of Chickamauga, General Grant was placed in command of all the Union forces in the West. Simultaneously, Rosecrans was replaced by General Thomas.

On October 23 Grant reached Chattanooga. Upon his arrival he was presented with a plan to open up a new supply line over Raccoon Mountain. General Hooker, who had arrived with several thousand men, was on the north bank of the river, several miles to the west. The plan was for him to cross the river and fight his way to Brown's Ferry where, simultaneously, a pontoon bridge was to be built. Supplies could then be brought over Raccoon Mountain and across the river on the new bridge. General Grant approved the plan and ordered it executed immediately. Only five days after his arrival, the bridge had been built; Hooker was in position guarding the new road, and the problem of supplies for Chattanooga had been solved. Now it was only a question of time before Sherman would arrive and the Union forces would be ready to fight their way out of the city to the south.

With all of these Union troops collected at Chattanooga, and with Sherman coming with additional divisions to oppose him, General Bragg made the incredible mistake of dividing his army and sending part of it away. General Longstreet, with his whole corps and some other troops attached, was ordered to east Tennessee to besiege Burnside at Knoxville. This move may have frightened some people, but it did not disturb General Grant who calmly went ahead with his plans to break out of Chattanooga. It simply meant that the job ahead would be that much easier.

The Confederate forces occupied the two prominent mountain ranges and the valley between them. Their right flank was on Missionary Ridge, their left on Lookout Mountain. At the time of the battle these two positions, now attractive residential areas, contained only a very few houses and were heavily wooded in places. Missionary Ridge, to the southeast of the city, is a long mountain range rising some two hundred feet above the plain. The Confederate troops were in three lines on the ridge; at the crest, at about the middle of the slope, and at the foot of the ridge. There was also an outpost line between the ridge and the city. The Confederate left rested on Lookout Mountain, rising abruptly some fifteen hundred feet above the plain (over twenty-one hundred feet above sea level). Although it is today a magnificent, scenic attraction, its rocky, rugged slopes presented a very serious military obstacle.

On November 15 General Sherman arrived in Chattanooga in advance of his troops to study the part he was to take in the coming battle. He found that General Grant planned to assault Missionary Ridge, ignoring Lookout Mountain. Sherman was to march his army completely around the north of the city. The woods and hills on the north bank of the river would conceal this movement. He was to cross the river and capture the north end of Missionary Ridge by a surprise attack. General Thomas, in the center of the Union line, was then to advance from the vicinity of the city, unite his forces with Sherman's, and drive to the south.

General Sherman was supposed to attack by November 21, but heavy rains made this impossible. In addition, the pontoon bridge at Brown's Ferry had broken, and one of his divisions had been left with General Hooker on the opposite flank near Lookout Mountain. This changed the plan considerably; it not only gave Sherman less of a striking force but also increased Hooker's strength to such a point that he, too, could be expected to take an active part in the battle. For the first time, the Confederate left flank on Lookout Mountain was included in the Union attack plan.

While Sherman was still getting into position, General Grant received reports that the Confederates were intending to retreat. He ordered the troops in the center to attack the position to their immediate front. This was one way to determine for sure whether or not General Bragg was retreating.

The battles around Chattanooga then developed in three successive phases, on three separate days. We could call November 23, 1863, the Battle of Orchard Knob, November 24 the Battle of Lookout Mountain, and November 25 the Battle of Missionary Ridge.

The first attack, the Battle of Orchard Knob, developed the fact that the Confederates were definitely not retreating. It was really only the outpost line in front of Missionary Ridge that was captured that day, but it proved to be an excellent point of departure for the Union attack that later carried the ridge itself.

The Battle of Lookout Mountain has become famous because of its picturesque location and also because of its other, poetic name of "The Battle above the Clouds." In actual fact the battle was not fought at the top of the mountain "above the clouds" but was fought in a heavy mist on a wooded, rocky slope about five hundred feet below the crest. The rugged character of the terrain and the thickness of the mist hampered both sides, but there was never any serious doubt as to the outcome. Hooker's force outnumbered the Confederates about six to one. The greater part of the action centered around Craven's House where the Confederates made their final stand, withdrawing after dark to Missionary Ridge. The next day a detachment planted the Stars and Stripes on top of Lookout Mountain.

On the same day that this engagement took place, General Sherman crossed the river and made his surprise attack on the north end of Missionary Ridge. It was a surprise, all right—to the Union army. The hill mass that he captured is in the general area of what is known today as Battery Heights. It is detached from Missionary Ridge itself, separated from it by a wide depression. His troops had not captured the north end of the ridge on the flank of the Confederate army but only a separate hill. He would still have to attack, uphill, the next day. Furthermore, at this point Missionary Ridge was steep and difficult to climb, and was being entrenched, even then, by the Confederates. Cleburne's Division of Hardee's Corps was occupying that next hill, throwing up breastworks of logs and dirt.

On November 25 was fought the decisive battle for Missionary Ridge. It started with Sherman's attack on Cleburne's Division. From early in the morning until the middle of the afternoon the Union troops maintained their assault, stubbornly refusing to admit that with six divisions they could not dislodge one Confederate division. They learned that determined defenders, well fortified by entrenchments, can withstand almost any attack. And Cleburne's men were determined. In some places the ridge was so steep that their cannon could not shoot downhill. They rolled boulders and cannonballs down on the attackers. After hours of fierce hand-to-hand combat the Union troops sullenly withdrew.

Sherman's main attack had failed, repulsed by Cleburne's outnumbered division. Where was Hooker who was supposed to move forward from Lookout Mountain and attack the other flank? There was no sign of his approach. At this point Grant ordered the troops in the center of his line to take the trenches at the foot of the ridge, but there to stop and await orders. General Thomas' men pushed forward but did not stop. Having taken the first line they found themselves completely exposed to firing from on top of the ridge. Against orders they started up and, to everyone's amazement,

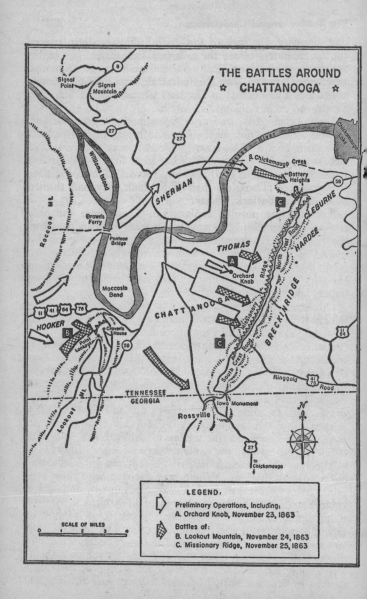

THE BATTLES AROUND
☆ CHATTANOOGA ☆

Signal Point

Signal Mountain

8

27

Williams Island

RACCOON MT.

Brown's Ferry

Pontoon Bridge

Moccasin Bend

27

SHERMAN

TENNESSEE RIVER

S. Chickamauga Creek

Battery Heights

C

58

Chickamauga Lake

North Creek Road

CLEBURNE

HARDEE

THOMAS

A

Orchard Knob

Missionary Ridge

BRECKINRIDGE

CHATTANOOGA

C

11 41 64 78

HOOKER

B

Point Lookout

Craven's House

58

Lookout MT.

South Crest Road

11 84

Ringgold

41 78 Road

TENNESSEE
GEORGIA

Rossville

Iowa Monument

N

27

To Chickamauga

LEGEND:

⇨ Preliminary Operations, including:
A. Orchard Knob, November 23, 1863

▨ Battles of:
B. Lookout Mountain, November 24, 1863
C. Missionary Ridge, November 25, 1863

SCALE OF MILES
0 1 2 3

kept climbing. Up and up the steep hills they went, sweeping the defenders before them in headlong flight. The battle was suddenly and dramatically finished an hour after Thomas' men surged forward. The Confederates, except for Cleburne's troops and a few others in Hardee's Corps, were in headlong flight.

Never before this, and never afterward, did the Confederate Army of Tennessee succumb to panic. These were veterans of many a desperate battle. What had happened? It is true they were heavily outnumbered but they had not fled on the preceding day at Lookout Mountain under similar circumstances. Then, on their right flank they had thrown back Sherman's attacks all day.

There is one possible explanation. These were the only soldiers on either side in any battle who for two days had been able to see the enemy gathering. From the top of this ridge with its panoramic view of the city, they had watched while the Union army prepared for attack. They could count the thousands who so heavily outnumbered them and then watch the whole blue mass charging upward, straight at every one of them. It was too much for the strongest nerves of the bravest veterans. These men were to fight again against as great numbers, but this time they could not.

The next day the victorious Union army undertook a vigorous pursuit. They might have captured all of the Confederate artillery and wagons but for one Confederate division which stopped the pursuit. Pat Cleburne and his men held off the Union troops until the rest of the army could escape in safety.

Casualties in the Battles around Chattanooga were not too severe. The Union forces, numbering close to 60,000, lost about 5800 men, of which 4700 were wounded. The Confederate army, which had about 37,000 present for duty, sustained approximately 6700 casualties but of these over 4100 were either captured or missing, which is sometimes a polite way of saying they went home, to return to the colors at a later date. It was Bragg's last battle; President Davis appointed General Joseph E. Johnston to take command.

From the Battles around
Chattanooga to Atlanta

IMMEDIATELY after the victory at Chattanooga, General Grant dispatched a large force to the relief of Knoxville, where Burnside's Army of the Ohio was being besieged by Longstreet's Corps. Three days before the Union troops arrived, the Confederates made an unsuccessful assault upon the city. Then, learning of the approach of reinforcements, they moved to near the North Carolina border, where Longstreet went into winter quarters, later rejoining General Lee in Virginia.

The first important action of the new year, 1864, was the occupation of Jacksonville, Florida, by Union troops early in February. A few days later they attempted to proceed farther inland but were defeated and withdrew, contenting themselves with occupying the city.

The next event of the new year was to prove most significant. Congress revived the grade of lieutenant general, previously held only by General George Washington, Winfield Scott having had the rank only by brevet. On March 9, at the White House, Ulysses S. Grant was handed his commission as lieutenant general and on the following day was assigned, by executive order, to command the armies of the United States. Two days later General Grant issued orders assigning Sherman to command in the West. Major General James B. McPherson was appointed to lead Sherman's army. General Halleck was retained as Grant's chief of staff in Washington, which did not mean command as it does today. Halleck actually became a coordinator and a liaison between Grant and his army commanders—Grant was determined not to remain in the political atmosphere of the capital. He planned to take the field, and did so, with the Army of the Potomac. Halleck also, therefore, served as a liaison between the President and General Grant.

In addition to these appointments, there was one other important change of leaders. The new commanding general was not satisfied with the past performance of the cavalry of the Army of the Potomac. Major General Philip H. Sheridan was called from command of an infantry division in the West to put new life into the cavalry of the East.

While Grant was still in the process of reorganizing the Union armies, an expedition which he did not favor was already under way up the Red River toward Shreveport, Louisiana. The officer in command of this force was Major General Nathaniel P. Banks, the same man who two years before had been so badly defeated by Stonewall Jackson in the Valley Campaign. This time his luck was no better. He captured Alexandria but was defeated by a Confederate force under Major General Richard Taylor on April 8. This ill-fated expedition was the last major effort west of the Mississippi by either side.

As mentioned above, General Grant did not approve of the Red River campaign. He was anxious to see it come to an end so that he could concentrate on the area east of the Mississippi. He was fully aware of the prime importance of this half of the Confederacy, where the munitions plants, and the two armies to protect them, were located. So, for the first time since the beginning of the war, a concerted plan of action was evolved for all the Union forces. General Sherman was to march into the heart of this section and engage Joseph E. Johnston's army in battle. Simultaneously, Meade was to move against Lee's army. Grant would accompany Meade. These two campaigns, to Atlanta and to Richmond and Petersburg, will be described more fully.

In addition to these main armies there were other forces engaged. As a part of Grant's over-all plan a Union army was to advance through the Valley of Virginia. This effort had only reached New Market when, on May 15, it was attacked and thoroughly defeated. The battle is particularly famous because the cadet corps of the Virginia Military Institute took part. These youthful soldiers fought magnificently, add-

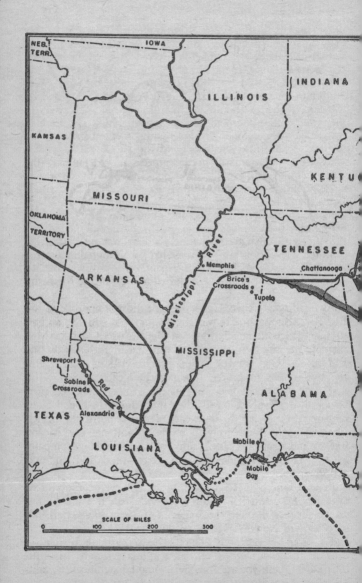

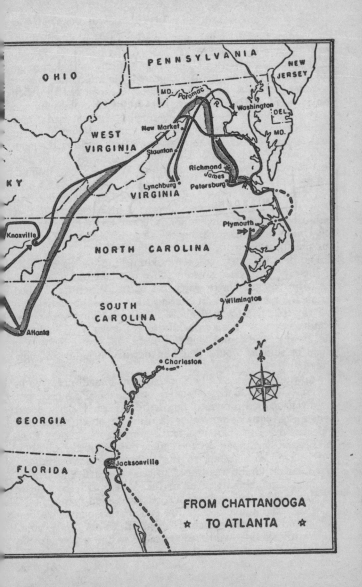

FROM CHATTANOOGA
★ TO ATLANTA ★

ing greatly to the honor and prestige of that fine military academy.

The next month the Union troops again started through the Valley. This time they captured Staunton and moved toward Lynchburg. In this emergency, General Lee detached the Second Corps of his army from the defense of Richmond to save the Valley. Under the command of Jubal Early, now a temporary lieutenant general, they arrived at Lynchburg in time to save the city. The next move was startling. General Early marched toward Washington. On July 11 he reached Fort Stevens, near the present site of Walter Reed Hospital, just five miles north of the White House. The people were sure that the nation's capital was about to be captured but General Early knew better. There was little chance of that with his small force. Furthermore, General Grant had detached the Union Sixth Corps from the siege of Richmond, and it was already arriving.

The next day there was some skirmishing on the outskirts of the city. President Lincoln drove out and was invited by the corps commander to watch the battle. When he climbed up on the parapet of Fort Stevens his tall, gaunt figure with the stovepie hat towered above all others. The corps commander began to plead with him to get down. It is said that the President did not descend until he was told that a squad of soldiers would pull him down. Then he smilingly agreed.

Knowing that his small army could not remain near Washington, General Early retreated across the Potomac, but his diversion had produced the desired effect. He had saved Lynchburg, cleared the Valley of Virginia of Union troops, and caused a large part of Grant's army to move away from the siege of Richmond. By the end of this period the situation had become so alarming to the authorities in Washington that General Grant was forced to send General Sheridan to command the Union forces in the Valley and to increase his strength by the addition of a second Union corps.

In the East, therefore, at the end of this period we find Grant and Lee facing each other at Richmond and Petersburg, with Sheridan and Early engaged in the Valley. In the West a somewhat similar situation had developed. The main campaign was, of course, Sherman's advance to Atlanta, but farther to the west there were subsidiary operations.

In the early part of the year before Sherman started his march toward Atlanta there had been some campaigning in Mississippi and a raid by General Forrest into Tennessee. By this time the name of Nathan Bedford Forrest, now a major general, had become so famous that he symbolized the entire Confederate effort in Mississippi and West Tennessee. Although he was not yet the commander in this area, it was decided that he must be defeated at all costs.

The first Union attempt ended at the Battle of Brice's Crossroads on June 10, where Forrest soundly defeated a numerically superior Union force in a battle which is considered to be one of the most outstanding examples of brilliant tactics in American military history.

The second Union effort ended near Tupelo on July 14 and 15. In this battle the Confederates attacked the Union forces commanded by Major General Andrew J. Smith but were repulsed. Although Smith subsequently retreated because he had exhausted his supplies, this victory was hailed throughout the North as a personal defeat for Forrest. This only serves to illustrate the magic of his name, because, although he was present, the senior Confederate commander was Major General Stephen D. Lee. Shortly afterward, Lee was called to Atlanta. General Forrest assumed command in northern Mississippi.

The third Union effort, again conducted by Major General Smith, ended in failure when Forrest slipped past the Union army and raided Union headquarters at Memphis. Smith was hastily recalled. This was the last attempt to catch General Forrest until the following year.

While these operations were taking place in the interior, other important events occurred on the Atlantic and Gulf coasts. Throughout this period the defenses of the city of Charleston were attacked several times. During this semisiege a Union ship was sunk by a submersible torpedo boat. The entire crew of this early submarine were drowned. All of them were volunteers who knew beforehand that they were going to certain death.

In April the Confederates delivered a joint land and naval attack against Plymouth, North Carolina. The new ironclad *Albemarle* defeated the wooden gunboats in the river while the army forces captured the town.

The most important naval event of the year was the action

in Mobile Bay on August 5 when Admiral Farragut destroyed the Confederate fleet. His famous "Damn the torpedoes. Go ahead." is as much a part of our naval tradition as the famous "Don't give up the ship!" from the war of 1812.

The Virginia Campaign of 1864

A TOTAL of four armies were involved in this campaign. The two Union forces were Meade's Army of the Potomac and the Army of the James. The latter was commanded by Major General Benjamin F. Butler, an incompetent officer whom Grant would have very much liked to replace but whose appointment was considered to be a political necessity. The over-all plan was for Meade to advance southward toward Richmond while Butler came up the James River to attack from the southeast.

The two Confederate forces were Lee's Army of Northern Virginia and an army hastily gathered to protect Richmond from Butler's advance. The command of this second force was given to General Beauregard.

Both Union armies started moving on May 4. General Butler's part in this campaign can be quickly told. His army of about 35,000 men advanced as far as Drewry's Bluff on the James River, south of Richmond, where on May 16 he was attacked by Beauregard with a force of about 25,000 men. Butler promptly withdrew and entrenched a line between the James and Appomattox Rivers. General Beauregard then constructed a parallel line and the Army of the James was thus effectively blocked, or as General Grant expressed it, contained "as if it has been in a bottle strongly corked."

The main campaign was between Lee's Army of Northern Virginia numbering about 62,000 men and Meade's Army of the Potomac, approximately 110,000 strong. General Grant, although in command of all the Union armies, clearly recognized the fact that General Lee was his main opponent, and therefore stayed with Meade's army. For all practical purposes, therefore, this campaign was actually Grant versus Lee.

The campaign opened shortly after midnight May 3-4. General Grant hoped that by marching at night his army might get through the Wilderness without having to fight in that tangled mass of undergrowth. General Lee had, however, anticipated that the Union forces would try to turn his right flank and marched to meet them. The result was two days of most furious and confused fighting under terrible conditions. It was impossible to see to control troop movements. The woods caught on fire. Men fought blindly on, sometimes unable to distinguish friend from foe, while the wounded perished in the flames. Here for the second time in the history of the Confederate Army a corps commander was shot by mistake by his own men. It is a strange coincidence that almost exactly one year after Stonewall Jackson's fatal wounding, General Longstreet was also shot while on reconnaissance. Both accidents occurred on almost the same ground and, in both cases, the generals concerned had just completed successful attacks on the Union forces. Longstreet recovered, but it was nearly six months before he could return to duty.

Always before at the end of such a hard-fought battle, when it had been partially defeated, the Army of the Potomac had retreated. For the first time in its history it advanced instead. On the night of May 7, General Grant marched by his left flank toward Spotsylvania, but when he arrived he found Lee's army entrenched across his path. During the next twelve days several assaults were made upon the Confederate defenses. The Union losses mounted higher and higher. They were much greater than those of the Confederates, but the Union forces had replacements, while Lee's army was steadily growing weaker, for there were too few men left in the South to fill his ranks.

While this battle was in progress Grant gave Sheridan permission to make a raid around the Confederate army. Jeb Stuart followed in pursuit. When Sheridan headed for Richmond, Stuart by a hard march managed to forestall him. On May 11 a fierce battle was fought at Yellow Tavern, north of Richmond. Jeb Stuart was mortally wounded and his command defeated. His death was a great blow to the Confederacy.

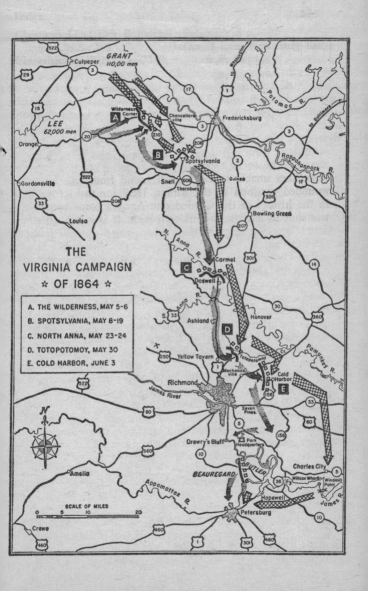

THE
VIRGINIA CAMPAIGN
☆ OF 1864 ☆

A. THE WILDERNESS, MAY 5-6
B. SPOTSYLVANIA, MAY 8-19
C. NORTH ANNA, MAY 23-24
D. TOTOPOTOMOY, MAY 30
E. COLD HARBOR, JUNE 3

GRANT 110,00 men

LEE 62,000 men

SCALE OF MILES
0   5   10   20

Grant decided again to march by his left flank and again the movement was started at night. In no other campaign of the war was there so much marching during darkness. It was getting to be standard practice for the Union army to march by night and fight by day. At the North Anna River Grant again found Lee in front of him. There was some skirmishing but no assault. Then for the fourth time Grant moved by his left flank only to find Lee waiting for him at Totopotomoy Creek. Another movement brought the forces together at Cold Harbor. Here, on June 3, General Grant decided to make a supreme effort to finish the Confederate army. The result was an assault in which the Union forces lost about 6000 men in one hour, of which probably one-third were killed. There is no doubt that this attack should never have been made. General Grant always regretted his decision of that day. Certainly, for the Union army, it was the low point in the campaign.

General Grant decided to move once more by his left flank and this time he finally surprised General Lee who thought he was moving to join Butler's force. Grant's true objective was Petersburg, twenty-three miles south of Richmond. He planned a combined move by Meade's Army of the Potomac and part of Butler's Army of the James to surprise the small garrison there. Possession of this city would cut Lee's supply route to the south and undoubtedly cause him to evacuate Richmond.

To effect the crossing of the James River the Union army constructed the longest continuous pontoon bridge ever used in the history of warfare. The river was 2,100 feet wide. The bridge, consisting of 101 pontoons, was layed in the amazingly short time of eight hours. The subsequent attack on Petersburg will be described later.

The Campaign to Atlanta

THE opposing forces in this campaign were of about the same strengths as Grant's and Lee's armies in Virginia. Both operations started early in May of 1864. But there the similarity ends. Grant's was a campaign of constant hammering. This was a campaign of skillful maneuvering in which the commanding generals of both armies proved that they possessed extraordinary ability.

General Sherman's Union forces consisted of three armies: the Army of the Cumberland, under Thomas; the Army of the Tennessee, under McPherson; and the Army of the Ohio, under Schofield. The first-named was by far the largest of the three, totaling 60,000 men. The second contained some 25,000 and was twice as large as the third. The total strength, including the cavalry, was about 110,000.

General Joseph E. Johnston's Army of Tennessee contained two corps, commanded by Hardee and Hood, of about 20,000 men each. A few days after the campaign opened they were joined by Polk's Army of Mississippi which, for all practical purposes, became a third, though somewhat smaller, corps. The total Confederate force, including the cavalry, was about 65,000 men.

In this campaign the Union troops had two prime objectives. The first was, of course, Johnston's armies. The second was the city of Atlanta which was, next to Richmond, the most important manufacturing center in the South. Its capture would reduce materially the Confederacy's ability to wage war.

The Confederates may be said to have had three objectives in this campaign. The first was, as always, the defeat of the Union armies. Being so heavily outnumbered, Johnston believed that his only hope of accomplishing this was to catch his opponent in a mistake and in the meantime to preserve his forces intact so that they would be capable of taking advantage of this opportunity when it arose. The second objective was the defense of Atlanta. The third was to stall for time as long as possible so that the war might appear to the North to be too costly. If President Lincoln were defeated at the polls in the forthcoming elections in November because of this, the war might be stopped. So long as there was any hope at all the Southern armies refused to admit defeat.

At the beginning of the campaign the Confederates occupied a very strong position on a commanding ridge of hills near Dalton, Georgia. It was so heavily fortified that Sherman decided not to assault it. He sent Thomas and Schofield to make a demonstration in front while McPherson's army marched on a wide turning movement to the south. Everything proceeded according to plan until McPherson arrived near Resaca where he encountered a small Confederate force which resisted so vigorously that the Union army halted.

General Sherman then moved south with most of his troops. Recognizing the danger to his left flank, General Johnston retired to Resaca where he was joined by Polk's Army of Mississippi. On May 14 the Union forces made a partial attack on this position. The following day the fighting was resumed, coupled with a movement over the Oostanaula River around Johnston's left flank, which caused the Confederates to again march southward.

General Johnston hoped to find suitable defensive positions at Calhoun and also at Adairsville, but in each case was disappointed. When near Cassville he discovered an opportunity to turn and attack the Union armies which were then advancing on a very broad front. Johnston decided to assault the Union left but the plan miscarried due to a mistake on the part of General Hood. Conceiving the notion that he was himself being outflanked, he halted his corps. This mistaken idea was caused by a small Union force that had taken the wrong road and was lost. The retreat continued to Allatoona.

The pass through the hills at this point was practically im-

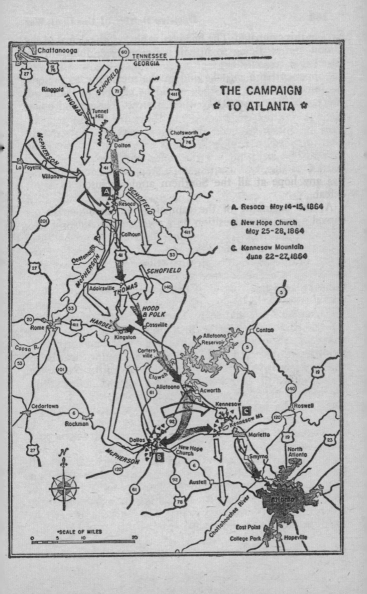

THE CAMPAIGN
✿ TO ATLANTA ✿

A. Resaca May 14-15, 1864

B. New Hope Church
   May 25-28, 1864

C. Kennesaw Mountain
   June 22-27, 1864

SCALE OF MILES
0   5   10   20

pregnable and could easily have been held against all assaults. General Sherman was keenly aware of its defensive possibilities, having traveled through it several years before. He therefore decided to undertake another wide flanking movement, marching south to Dallas, but upon arrival he found Johnston waiting at New Hope Church. There followed three days of sharp skirmishing to develop the Confederate position, culminating in an unsuccessful attempt on May 27 to turn Johnston's right flank. Sherman then decided to swing back to his left again but the movement was delayed by a fierce Confederate assault delivered on May 28 against the Union right.

Then began a series of operations which eventually brought Sherman's troops in line in front of Kennesaw Mountain. It was during this period that "Bishop" Polk's dream of returning to the ministry was ended. On June 14 he was killed instantly by a long-range shot from a Union battery.

Up until now, although the advance had carried over three-fourths of the distance to Atlanta, there had not actually been a large-scale battle between the two forces. There was a growing feeling of unrest and dissatisfaction among the Union officers and men. They wanted to fight and end the campaign. They knew they outnumbered the Confederates and they were tired of marching back and forth from left to right. Furthermore it had been raining heavily for the last few days and the roads were in terrible condition. Faced with a decision between an assault and another turning movement, Sherman on June 27 loosed his forces upon the Confederate positions. The attack was a valiant effort, bravely executed, but it was severely repulsed, proving to everyone that frontal assault upon a fortified strong-point could not defeat such a determined enemy.

The Union forces then moved by their right flank south as far as the Chattahoochee River. Retreating from one position to another, the Confederate armies eventually retired across the river to a strong position just north of Atlanta. Here, on July 17, General Johnston was relieved from command by order of President Davis.

The Battles around Atlanta

THE decision to relieve General Joseph E. Johnston from command at this time was due to the popular outcry at his having retreated so far without having made serious efforts to attack the Union forces. President Davis gave the command to John B. Hood, appointing him a temporary full general.

To say the least, the change was not popular. The officers and men of the Confederate armies knew Hood as an aggressive, impetuous fighter, an excellent division or corps commander, but they were very doubtful of his ability to lead them to victory against such a foe as they now faced. They gave him unquestioned obedience but they were afraid that President Davis overrated his ability. None doubted his bravery—he had lost an arm at Gettysburg and a leg at Chickamauga—but they questioned his judgment. Furthermore, it was asking a great deal of a man so physically disabled and probably in constant pain to assume so responsible a command.

One man was pleased—General Sherman. He had an exceptionally high opinion of Johnston's ability and now knew that at last the Confederates would come out from behind their entrenchments. In open warfare the superior Northern numbers should count far more. At this time the Union armies had swung to the east. McPherson and Schofield were making a wide flanking movement with McPherson on the outside, approaching Atlanta from the northeast. Thomas with his three corps was approaching from the north. There was a large gap between Schofield and Thomas so one corps had been sent eastward to close it. This had left another gap between it and the remaining two corps. Furthermore, Thomas was then in the process of crossing Peachtree Creek (where the Bobby Jones Golf Course is now) which was then very wide and marshy.

General Hood determined to take advantage of this situation. He gave one of his corps the mission of holding McPherson and Schofield while he attacked Thomas at Peachtree Creek with the rest of the Confederate army. Unfortunately for the attackers, their timing was a little late. Thomas had been able to get enough of his troops across and had formed them on the ridge along which Collier Road runs today. The attack of July 20 was repulsed with heavy losses. General Hood withdrew his forces into the entrenchments already prepared for the defense of Atlanta.

After such a severe repulse the Union commanders did not expect another attack. In fact General Sherman received information that led him to believe that Atlanta was being evacuated. He issued orders for a pursuit. When Hood struck again the surprise was complete.

On the night of July 21, General Hardee was sent on a long march of fifteen miles around the left and rear of the Union forces. His assault was to be supported by a frontal attack. About noon on the 22nd Hardee struck McPherson's army with tremendous force. This attack was launched near the present Moreland Avenue (U.S. Highway 23) and Flat Shoals Road. If Hood had moved Cheatham's Corps forward at the same time the result would surely have been a resounding Union defeat. Hood's plan had been bold and Hardee had executed it brilliantly. Again, it was the timing that failed. The flank attack had spent itself before the frontal attack was launched. This also was delivered with vigor and great bravery but it was about three hours too late. Some of the Union troops were actually able to fight off the first assault, then turn and help repulse the second. With simultaneous attacks this would have been impossible. In the Battle of Atlanta the Confederates again suffered far more severe casualties than the Union forces. The Army of the Tennessee, however, lost its great leader, General McPherson, whom both Grant and Sherman considered to be one of the most outstanding officers in the service.

The Union forces now drew their lines closely around

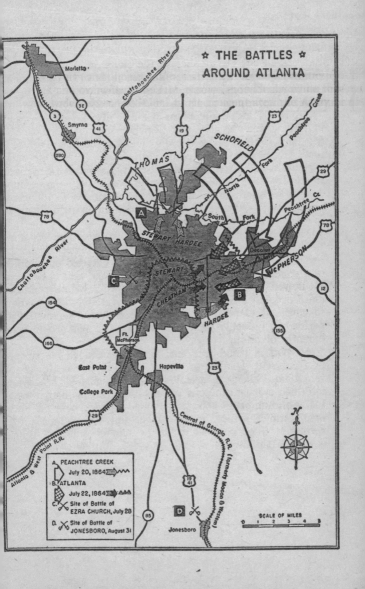

☆ THE BATTLES ☆
AROUND ATLANTA

Marietta

Chattahoochee River

Smyrna

SCHOFIELD

Peachtree Creek

THOMAS

Fort

North

Chattahoochee River

STEWART HARDEE

A

South   Fort

Peachtree Ck.

Decatur

McPHERSON

STEWART

C

CHEATHAM

B

HARDEE

Ft. McPherson

East Point

Hapeville

College Park

Central of Georgia R.R. (formerly Macon & Western)

N

Atlanta & West Point R.R.

SCALE OF MILES
0 1 2 3 4 5

A. PEACHTREE CREEK
   July 20, 1864
B. ATLANTA
   July 22, 1864
C. Site of Battle of
   EZRA CHURCH, July 28
D. Site of Battle of
   JONESBORO, August 31

Jonesboro

Atlanta and began at the same time to move to their right.
The object was to strike at the Atlanta and West Point
Railroad to cut off supplies to the city from the southwest.
On July 28 the Confederates attacked this turning movement
near Ezra Church, where Mozley Park is today, and again
were severely repulsed.

After this battle there was a long delay before Sherman
moved again. The city was heavily bombarded for several
days at a time. Cavalry was dispatched to break up the railroads to the south but accomplished very little. One such
expedition met with complete disaster. Its purpose had been
to release 34,000 soldiers held at Andersonville, nearly a hundred miles south of Atlanta, the largest of the Confederate
prison camps. Almost all of the Union cavalrymen involved
in this raid were themselves captured.

Meanwhile, Sherman had been slowly extending his lines
to the right, but as fast as he did so Hood extended his to
the left. Finally, late in August, Sherman started on another
of his wide turning movements around to the west of Atlanta.
He moved very slowly and spent an entire day destroying the
railroad line. This delay and some misleading information
so confused General Hood that he thought Sherman had
decided to retreat. A grand victory ball was planned to cele-
brate the occasion.

As soon as Hood recovered from this strange misconcep-
tion he sent Hardee to attack the enveloping forces at
Jonesboro. When this assault failed on August 31, Hood was
forced to evacuate the city or be surrounded. Although eventually outnumbered about six to one, Hardee held off Sherman's armies while Hood escaped, and then joined forces
with him three days later. On September 2 Union troops
entered Atlanta.

From the Battles around Atlanta
to Appomattox

THE capture of Atlanta practically assured the re-election of President Lincoln. His party could now show that something definite had actually been accomplished in 1864. When the Union forces successfully completed another campaign in the Valley of Virginia in the following month, just twenty days before the election, there was no doubt whatever of the outcome.

On September 19 General Sheridan advanced against the Confederates in the Valley and defeated them in the Third Battle of Winchester. General Early retreated, pursued by the Union forces. After clearing the Confederates from most of the Valley, Sheridan turned back. As he retired slowly northward, his soldiers systematically and thoroughly destroyed all sources of food in the region. The Valley of Virginia, which had been the granary supplying Lee's army, was completely stripped of all supplies.

Although outnumbered at least two to one, Early followed and on October 19 made a surprise attack on the Union forces at Cedar Creek. Then, with victory in their grasp, the famished Confederate soldiers were permitted to stop and forage for supplies. Sheridan had not been present at the beginning of the battle. Galloping on the scene he helped rally the retreating soldiers and led the counterattack to victory. This ride to battle has been immortalized by "Sheridan's Ride," a spirited poem, but inaccurate in that he did not actually gallop as many as twenty miles. The Union victory was decisive. It was the last great battle fought in the Valley.

Before returning to the West to follow the campaigns in that region, the exploit of Lieutenant William B. Cushing of the United States Navy should be told. On the night of October 27 he and a small crew in a steam launch slipped past the Confederate lookouts to Plymouth, North Carolina. Their target was the ironclad ram *Albemarle*. Though discovered at the last minute, they managed to explode a torpedo against the side of the ship, sinking it. Cushing and one other man escaped.

After the capture of Atlanta, Sherman and his armies remained inactive for a month. No attempt was made to pursue the Confederate forces. Late in September General Hood took the initiative. He realized that the Union troops were having trouble maintaining their line of communications, stretching well over four hundred miles to the northwest. More men than ever before were needed to guard them. Now Hood decided to attack those long lines of supply. Sending General Thomas back to Nashville to organize the defense from the North, Sherman remained in Atlanta to await developments.

On October 5 Hood struck at Allatoona. Eight days later he captured Dalton, then retired toward Alabama. Sherman pursued across the state line, but gave up the chase when he realized that he could not catch the Confederates. Now we find the unusual situation of two opposing armies moving in opposite directions, Hood marching westward, Sherman to the southeast. Detaching two of his corps to aid General Thomas in the defense of Tennessee, Sherman returned to Atlanta to begin his famous march to the sea.

In order to carry out his plan of marching to the Atlantic coast, General Sherman had to abandon Atlanta. But it was essential that the city not be returned to the Confederates, with all its war-making potential intact. The work of destruction was thoroughly done although the fire spread beyond the limits intended, burning about one-third of the city. Unfortunately, the lawless element to be found in any large community then took the opportunity of doing some burning of its own.

On November 15, having cut himself off from all communication with the North, Sherman started across Georgia with an army of over 60,000 men. Until they arrived on the coast, the people in the North could follow their movements only by reading the Southern newspapers. There was practically no opposition to the march. Along a path fifty to sixty miles wide, it cut right through the heart of the State, wrecking the railroad system, and destroying all supplies. That this march and his next one through the Carolinas shortened the war by many months is undeniable. These operations seriously damaged the wartime economy of the Confederacy; furthermore the very fact that the marches could be made with such ease was a great blow to the morale of the people of the South. On December 21 Sherman occupied Savannah.

Let us now turn back and follow Hood's campaign into Tennessee. Although his army reached Florence, Alabama, late in October, supply difficulties and heavy rains prevented any forward movement until the latter part of November. General Forrest, who was on a raid in west Tennessee destroying gunboats and transports along the Tennessee River, was ordered to join Hood's army but was also delayed by the heavy rains. The Union armies were greatly helped by Hood's slow start, for their forces were widely scattered and they needed time to assemble. The concentration had still not been completed when the Confederates advanced.

When he began his campaign General Hood had almost 40,000 men. Opposing him was a force of about 33,000 Union troops under Major General Schofield, whose mission was to gain time for General Thomas to assemble the greatest possible number of troops at Nashville. Schofield waited too long before starting to retreat. By a well-conceived maneuver General Hood placed his army in a position to cut off the Union retreat. At Spring Hill, Tennessee, many of the Confederate units were closer to Nashville than was Schofield, but then this great opportunity slipped from their grasp. By marching all night within earshot of the Confederate outposts, the Union forces reached Franklin and hastily entrenched. Hood's best chance of winning his Tennessee campaign was lost.

On the following day, November 30, the Confederates pursued to Franklin, where Hood made the fatal mistake of ordering an attack on the Union positions. It was a desperate

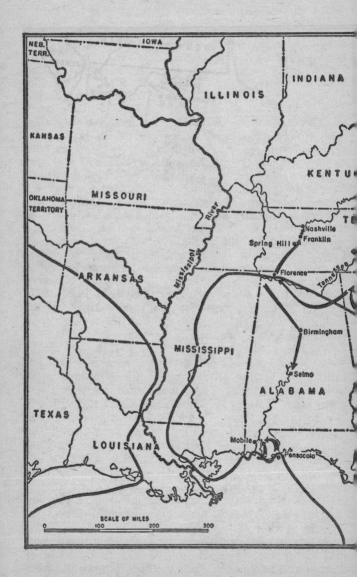

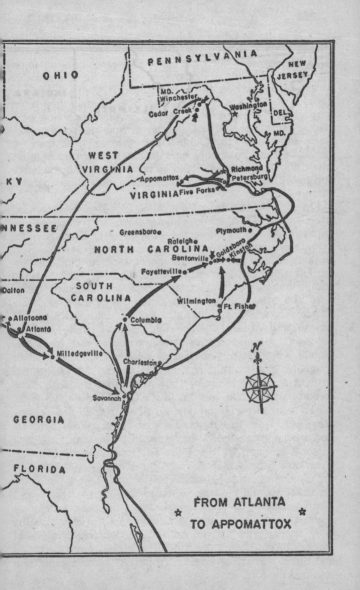

FROM ATLANTA
TO APPOMATTOX

gamble to try to prevent Schofield from escaping again, but should never have been attempted. The Confederate numerical superiority was not great enough to warrant an attack on an entrenched line. Furthermore, all of the Confederate army had not arrived on the battlefield. In spite of this, the assaults were so fiercely and gallantly made that they broke through the center of the line. Only the timely use of a reserve brigade saved the Union forces from destruction. The losses suffered by the Confederates were so great that the Battle of Franklin should have halted Hood's campaign. A total of more than 6000 men were casualties. Pat Cleburne and four other generals were killed; seven more were wounded or captured.

Despite the disaster at Franklin, Hood pushed forward to Nashville. Then, while Thomas slowly and carefully prepared for battle, Hood sent Forrest away to conduct other operations. For nearly two weeks Thomas waited, first to procure more horses for his cavalry, next for better weather. His slowness drew down upon him the wrath of the administration and of General Grant, who prepared to relieve him from command. On December 15 Thomas finally moved forward. The Union attack at the Battle of Nashville was so well planned and so well executed that the Confederates, outnumbered two to one, never had a chance. Hood's army fought bravely but could not hold. Instead of retreating that night, Hood formed a new line and stayed to fight again. This decision was brave, but foolhardy. The second day's battle was decisive. The Confederates were driven from the field and pursued all the way to the Tennessee River. Upon his return General Hood asked to be relieved from command. What was left of his army was sent to the Carolinas. This was the last active campaign in the West until March of 1865.

While the Battle of Nashville was being fought, a Union expedition was under way to capture Fort Fisher on the North Carolina coast. The army troops were under the command of Major General Butler, who so mismanaged the affair that the effort was an utter failure. After this convincing evidence of Butler's incompetence, even political necessity was overruled and Butler was at last relieved. In January another expedition captured the fort.

At this late hour the Confederate Congress passed a bill providing for a general in chief. The obvious choice was Robert E. Lee, and President Davis appointed him to the post on February 6, 1865. It was, of course, too late for the new commanding general to change the course of the war to any perceptible degree. The stage had been set for the final campaigns. General Sherman was already moving northward from Savannah. Another large force was collecting at Fort Fisher, preparing to join him in North Carolina.

In planning his march, General Sherman decided not to advance through Charleston. This city had been so damaged by bombardment that it was no longer a worthwhile objective. The capture of Columbia, the capital of South Carolina, would in any event force troops remaining in Charleston to withdraw.

The march of the Union army through this section of South Carolina was one of the most amazing feats of the war. They plunged straight through swamps that were considered impassable. One look at this country today and we can only wonder how it was done at all, yet Sherman's men averaged ten miles or more a day. On February 17 the Union troops entered Columbia to find that the departing Confederates had set fire to some cotton to keep it from falling into enemy hands. Before the flames could be extinguished about one half of the city had been burned.

By the end of the month, General Sherman was almost at the North Carolina border. In the meantime the Union troops operating from Fort Fisher had occupied Wilmington, North Carolina, and were preparing to move toward Goldsboro. To coordinate the efforts of the Southern forces against these two threats, General Lee called General Johnston from retirement. In doing so, both officers were well aware that Johnston's task of defending North Carolina was an impossible as was Lee's at Richmond and Petersburg.

In the month of March events moved rapidly. Johnston sent a force to engage one of the columns advancing inland from the coast. In a battle fought at Kinston on March 8, 9, and 10, the Confederates were repulsed and forced to withdraw. On the next day Sherman occupied Fayetteville. The final battle of the campaign in North Carolina occurred at Bentonville on March 19 when Johnston turned to strike a part of Sherman's army. The attack was at first successful, but when more Union troops appeared on the scene Johnston was forced on the defensive. Two days later he retreated from the battlefield, and Sherman moved forward to occupy Goldsboro, uniting with the troops coming from the coast.

The Siege of Petersburg

No history of the Civil War would be complete without some description of the nearly ten-month-long Siege of Petersburg. This city first became a target for the Union armies early in June, 1864. For the preceding month every effort by General Grant to defeat Lee's army or to capture Richmond, farther to the north, had been unsuccessful. Grant then decided to advance on Petersburg. If he could capture this city, the railroads supplying Richmond from the south would be cut and the Confederate capital would undoubtedly be evacuated.

At this time Petersburg was protected by a strong line of trenches constructed in 1862 and 1863 but its garrision consisted of only one Confederate brigade. General Beauregard, who was then responsible for the defense of the southern approaches to Richmond, had few troops to spare. Most of the men available were farther to the north across the Appomattox River facing General Butler and the Union Army of the James. (In describing the beginning of the Siege of Petersburg, we have been forced to turn back the calendar. Over six months have yet to elapse before General Butler is removed for incompetence.)

The first attempt to capture Petersburg was made by some of Butler's troops on June 9. It was a halfhearted affair that nevertheless would have succeeded but for the combined efforts of the one Confederate brigade and a hastily organized group of old men and boys from the city.

Six days later, on June 15, came General Grant's attack. It was supposed to have been delivered by the Eighteenth

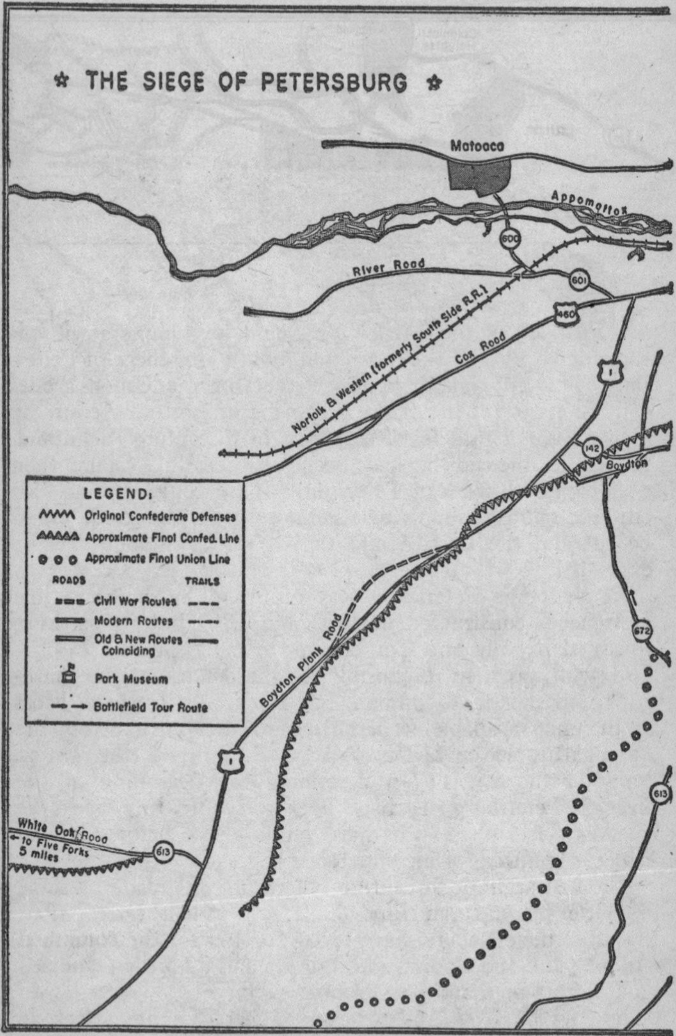

☆ THE SIEGE OF PETERSBURG ☆

Matoaca

Appomattox

River Road

Norfolk & Western (formerly South Side R.R.)

Cox Road

Boydton

LEGEND:

⋀⋀⋀⋀ Original Confederate Defenses
⋀⋀⋀⋀ Approximate Final Confed. Line
●●● Approximate Final Union Line

ROADS   TRAILS
━ ━ ━ Civil War Routes   ─ ─ ─
━━━ Modern Routes
━━━ Old & New Routes
          Coinciding

🏛 Park Museum

━●━ Battlefield Tour Route

Boydton Plank Road

White Oak Road
← to Five Forks
5 miles

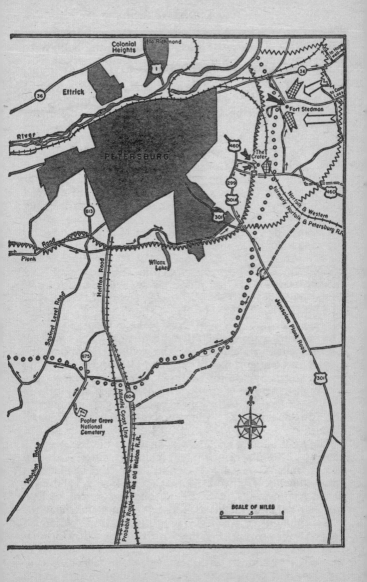

Corps (Butler's army) and the Second Corps of Meade's Army of the Potomac. Through various errors, both corps were slow in moving, and only the Eighteenth attacked. This assault was not made until 7:00 p.m. but captured a mile and a half of trenches. Then, learning of the arrival of Confederate reinforcements, the attack was suspended. On the following day the assault was renewed, and more of the Confederate lines were captured. By June 17 the whole Army of the Potomac had reached the battlefield and only a small part of the Army of Northern Virginia had arrived to reinforce Beauregard. Still the Confederate lines held and continued to hold on the following day when General Lee arrived to take command. General Beauregard and the few men he had with him, by their magnificent defense against overwhelming numbers, saved Petersburg.

On any one of these days from June 15 through June 18, the Union forces should have taken the city and General Grant's plan would have succeeded. For the first time he had completely misled General Lee who for three days had thought that most of the Union army was still far to the north. If the units on the field had made coordinated attacks, or attempted to maneuver to the south around Beauregard's position, Petersburg would certainly have fallen.

A condition of stabilization had now been reached. General Grant concluded that he could not capture the Confederate entrenchments by storm. He decided to operate against the railways to the south. During the next nine and a half months various efforts were made to reach around Lee's army to the south. Attempts were also made, at times, to concentrate quickly at various points of the line to break through.

The most unusual of these was known as the Battle of the Crater. The 48th Pennsylvania Infantry, composed largely of coal miners, dug a long tunnel under the Confederate entrenchments. The work was begun on June 25 and completed on July 23. One of the reasons that it took so long was that the army engineers were not enthusiastic about the venture and offered practically no assistance. It was performed under the supervision of the regimental commander, Lieutenant Colonel Henry Pleasants, a mining engineer in civil life. It went 511 feet into the earth, then had lateral galleries extending along the Confederate lines for an additional 75 feet, a

total of 586 feet. The charge was four tons of powder. There
is a scale model of the tunnel on display at the Park Museum
located near the site of the Crater.

The mine was to be exploded at 3:30 a.m., July 30. The
fuse was lit but nothing happened. Two men from the regiment crawled in, located the trouble, relit the fuse, and
managed to crawl out again before the mine exploded at 4:45
a.m. It blew a huge crater in the Confederate lines, at least
170 feet long, 60 feet wide, and 25 feet deep. The way was
now open for the Union army to penetrate the Confederate
defenses. The leading Union division charged forward, dived
into the crater and stayed there, except for the division commander who never stirred from the Union lines. Two more
divisions advanced, but many of these men also stayed in
the crater. More than an hour later they were joined by
most of the personnel of a colored division, whose commander also remained behind.

By now the Confederates had recovered from the shock
caused by the explosion. They poured artillery fire into the
confused, milling mob, and charged forward to restore their
lines. By early afternoon the battle was over. The best sum-
mary of the results came from General Grant, "It was the
saddest affair I have witnessed in the war. Such opportunity
for carrying fortifications I have never seen and do not expect
again to have."

General Lee's force was never invested. The war became one
of attrition, typical of what took place later in World War I.
The attackers continuously extended their lines to the
left, and Lee was forced to stretch his line to the utmost limit
until in February of 1865 he was holding a line of trenches
from north of Richmond to south of Petersburg, fifty-three
miles in length, one-ninth as long as the Western Front in
Europe in 1918.

On March 25 General Lee made one last assault against the
Union lines. Led by Lieutenant General John B. Gordon, the
Confederate troops moved silently forward and just before
dawn captured Fort Stedman. At daybreak the Union forces
reacted vigorously; Gordon's men were driven back and the
front restored.

Four days later General Grant began his last turning movement to the left. It ended in a victory by Sheridan at the
Battle of Five Forks on April 1. Grant immediately ordered a

general assault at dawn of April 2. The attack broke through the Confederate right. Hastening to the front to try to rally his men, General A. P. Hill was killed. That night the Army of Northern Virginia left Petersburg and Richmond on the road to Appomattox.

On April 9, Palm Sunday, Lee and Grant met at Appomattox to discuss the terms of surrender of Lee's Army of Northern Virginia. There were no more battles in the East. General Sherman moved forward to occupy Raleigh, North Carolina. On April 26, near Greensboro, General Johnston also surrendered his army. (See the map entitled "From Atlanta to Appomattox," on pages 204–205.)

While the main operations were coming to an end in the East, there had been two important campaigns conducted in Alabama. The first of these was an advance northward from the Gulf of Mexico. On March 17 two strong Union columns commanded by Major General Edward Canby moved against Mobile. Five days later a cavalry force led by Major General James H. Wilson started southward from the Tennessee River toward Birmingham (then called Elyton). On April 2 Wilson defeated Lieutenant General Forrest at Selma. Ten days afterward Mobile was occupied by General Canby's troops. The war in this region ended when Lieutenant General Richard Taylor surrendered to General Canby on May 4. The same officer received the surrender of all Confederate forces west of the Mississippi from General Kirby Smith on May 26.

After the lapse of nearly one hundred years it is sometimes difficult for us to realize the effect that the Civil War had upon the people of the United States. With the memory of World War II fresh in our minds, one simple comparison should serve to impress us with the magnitude and complexity of this conflict between the States. During the period of the Civil War the total population of the country, both North and South, was only about 31,000,000. During World War II we were a nation of approximately 130,000,000 people. Yet the total cost in American lives in our Civil War was more than twice as great.

To attempt to compare here the services rendered or the abilities of the soldiers of either side would be fruitless. Each side has its adherents who can prove their arguments on ground of their own choosing. One point should nevertheless be noted carefully. The greatest casualties suffered by this nation occurred in a war fought between her own sons. Americans do not desire war, but when called to engage in battle they have consistently proven that as a rabble in arms they are no better than any other; but when well trained and properly led they have made as capable fighting men as any in history. It is entirely sufficient to recall Trenton and Princeton; Chancellorsville, Gettysburg, Chickamauga, and Petersburg; Saint-Mihiel and the Meuse-Argonne; Normandy, the Ardennes, Leyte, and Iwo Jima.

Bibliography

A simple listing of the sources consulted would not be a fair or accurate method of reporting their value in the preparation of this book. It seems far better to divide the bibliography into two categories. Asterisks indicate those books or manuscripts which furnished the bulk of the information on which this book is based. The remaining entries consist of other sources from which a lesser amount of information was taken or which were used to cross-check the historical data presented herein, and which the reader is encouraged to consult for further information.

* Alexander, Brig. Gen. E. P., *Military Memoirs of a Confederate*. New York: Charles Scribner's Sons, 1907.
* Bigelow, John, Jr., *The Campaign of Chancellorsville*. New Haven: Yale University Press, 1910.
Boatner, Mark Mayo, III, *The Civil War Dictionary*. New York: David McKay Co., 1959.
Bradford, Gamaliel, *Lee, The American*. Boston: Houghton Mifflin Co., 1912.
Bruce, Robert V., *Lincoln and the Tools of War*. Indianapolis: The Bobbs-Merrill Co., 1956.
Catton, Bruce, *A Stillness at Appomattox*. New York: Doubleday & Co., 1952.
———— *Glory Road*. New York: Doubleday & Co., 1952.
———— *Mr. Lincoln's Army*. New York: Doubleday & Co., 1951.
———— *This Hallowed Ground*. New York: Doubleday & Co., 1956.

——————— U. S. Grant and the American Military Tradition. Boston: Little, Brown & Co., 1954.

Chamberlain, Joshua I., The Passing of the Armies. New York: G. P. Putnam's Sons, 1915.

Cullum, Maj. Gen. George W., Biographical Register of the Officers and Graduates of the U. S. Military Academy.

Davis, Jefferson, The Rise and Fall of the Confederate Government. New York: D. Appleton & Co., 1881. New York: Thomas Yoseloff, Inc., 1959.

Dictionary of American Biography, edited by Allen Johnson. New York: Charles Scribner's Sons, 1943.

Douglas, Henry Kyd, I Rode With Stonewall. Chapel Hill: University of North Carolina Press, 1940. New York: Fawcett Publications, 1961.

Eliot, Ellsworth, Jr., West Point in the Confederacy. New York: G. A. Baker & Co., 1941.

* Fieberger, Col. G. J., Campaigns of the American Civil War. West Point: United States Military Academy Printing Office, 1914.

* ——————— The Campaign and Battle of Gettysburg. West Point: United States Military Academy Press, 1915.

* Freeman, Douglas S., R. E. Lee: A Biography. New York: Charles Scribner's Sons, 1934-35.

* ——————— Lee's Lieutenants. New York: Charles Scribner's Sons, 1942-1944.

Geer, Walter, Campaigns of the Civil War. New York: Brentano's, 1926.

Gordon, Lt. Gen. John B., Reminiscences of the Civil War. New York: Charles Scribner's Sons, 1903.

Gosnell, Lt. Cmdr. H. Allen, Guns on the Western Waters. Baton Rouge: Louisiana State University Press, 1949.

Grant, Gen. Ulysses S., Personal Memoirs of U. S. Grant. New York: Charles L. Webster & Co., 1885-86. New York: Fawcett Publications, 1962, (Abridged).

* Henderson, Col. G. F. R., Stonewall Jackson and the American Civil War. New York: Longmans, Green & Co., 1932.

Henry, Ralph S., "First with the Most" Forrest. Indianapolis: The Bobbs-Merrill Co., 1944.

* Horn, Stanley F., The Army of Tennessee. Indianapolis: The Bobbs-Merrill Co., 1941.

* Humphreys, Maj. Gen. Andrew A., The Virginia Campaign of '64 & '65. New York: Charles Scribner's Sons, 1937.

* Johnson, Robert U. and Buel, Clarence C. (Eds.), Battles and Leaders of the Civil War. New York: The Century Co., 1884-1887.

Lee, Capt. Robert E., Recollections and Letters of General Robert E. Lee. New York: Doubleday, Page & Co., 1904. New York: Doubleday & Co., 1926.

Lewis, Lloyd, Sherman, Fighting Prophet. New York: Harcourt, Brace & Co., 1932.

Livermore, Thomas L., *Numbers and Losses in the Civil War in America, 1861-65.* Boston: Houghton Mifflin & Co., 1900. Bloomington: University of Indiana Press, 1958.

Longstreet, Lt. Gen. James, *From Manassas to Appomattox.* Philadelphia: J. B. Lippincott Company, 1896. Bloomington: University of Indiana Press, 1960.

Maurice, Maj. Gen. Sir Frederick, *Robert E. Lee, The Soldier.* Boston: Houghton Mifflin Co., 1925.

Miller, Francis Trevelyan, *The Photographic History of the Civil War.* 10 vols. New York: Review of Reviews Co., 1911. Reprinted in 5 vols., Henry Steele Commager, ed., New York: Thomas Yoseloff, Inc., 1957.

* Mitchell, Col. William A., *Outlines of the World's Military History.* Washington, D. C.: Infantry Journal, 1931.

Pemberton, John C., *Pemberton, Defender of Vicksburg.* Chapel Hill: The University of North Carolina Press, 1942.

* Ropes, John C., *The Story of the Civil War* (Completed By Col. William R. Livermore). New York: G. P. Putnam's Sons, 1933.

Schaff, Morris, *The Battle of the Wilderness.* Boston: Houghton Mifflin Co., 1910.

Shannon, Fred Albert, *The Organization and Administration of the Union Army: 1861-1865.* Chicago: Arthur H. Clark Co., 1928.

Sherman, Gen. William T., *Memoirs of General William T. Sherman.* New York: D. Appleton & Co., 1875. Bloomington: University of Indiana Press, 1957.

Sorrell, Brig. Gen. G. Moxley, *Recollections of a Confederate Staff Officer.* New York & Washington: The Neale Publishing Co., 1905.

* Steele, Maj. Matthew F., *American Campaigns* (United States Infantry Association, Washington, D. C.). Harrisburg, Pa.: The Telegraph Press, 1943.

Stephenson, Nathaniel W., *Abraham Lincoln and the Union.* New Haven: Yale University Press, 1918.

———— *The Day of the Confederacy.* New Haven: Yale University Press, 1919.

Storrick, W. C., *The Battle of Gettysburg.* Harrisburg: J. Horace McFarland Co., 1954.

Swinton, William, *The Twelve Decisive Battles of the War.* New York: Dick & Fitzgerald, 1873.

Thomas, Benjamin, *Abraham Lincoln.* New York: Alfred A. Knopf, 1952.

Thomason, Capt. John W., Jr., *Jeb Stuart.* New York: Charles Scribner's Sons, 1930.

Turner, George E., *Victory Rode the Rails.* Indianapolis: The Bobbs-Merrill Co., 1953.

Vandiver, Frank E., *Rebel Brass: The Confederate Command System.* Baton Rouge: The Louisiana State University Press, 1956.

Van Horne, Thomas B., *The Life of Major General George H. Thomas*. New York: Charles Scribner's Sons, 1882.

* War of the Rebellion, *Official Records of the Union and Confederate Armies*. War Department, Government Printing Office, 1880-1901.

* Williams, Kenneth P., *Lincoln Finds a General*. New York: The MacMillan Co., 1949-52.

Williams, T. Harry, *Lincoln and His Generals*. New York: Alfred A. Knopf, 1952.

Wise, Jennings C., *The Long Arm of Lee*. Lynchburg: J. P. Bell Co., 1913. New York: Oxford University Press, 1959.

* Wood, W. Birbeck and Edmonds, J. E., *A History of the Civil War in the United States, 1861-5*. New York: G. P. Putnam's Sons, 1905.

Wood, William, *Captains of the Civil War*. New Haven: Yale University Press, 1921.

Wyeth, John A., *Life of General Nathan Bedford Forrest*. New York: Harper & Brothers, 1904.

In addition to these, the late Col. Girard Lindsley McEntee's as yet unpublished *Military History of the Civil War* proved invaluable.

The various pamphlets published by the National Park Service, Department of the Interior, were helpful on many occasions in locating places on the map and on the ground.

Index